TIMES SQUARE

TIMES SQUARE

A PICTORIAL HISTORY

By Jill Stone

COLLIER BOOKS

A DIVISION OF MACMILLAN PUBLISHING CO., INC.

New York

Macmillan Publishing Co., Inc.
866 Third Avenue, New York, N.Y. 10022
Collier Macmillan Canada, Inc.

Library of Congress Cataloging in Publication Data

Stone, Jill.
Times Square : a pictorial history.

Includes index.
1. Times Square (New York, N.Y.)—History.
2. Times Square (New York, N.Y.)—Description.
3. New York (N.Y.)—History.   4. New York
(N.Y.)—Description.   I. Title.
F128.68.T55S76   1982   974.7′1   81-21741
ISBN 0-02-037730-4 (pbk.)   AACR2

First Collier Books Edition 1982
10 9 8 7 6 5 4 3 2 1

Times Square is also published in a hardcover edition by
Macmillan Publishing Co., Inc.

Printed in the United States of America

DESIGN BY RON FARBER

For my grandmother, who has always been there

Contents

Acknowledgments

I would like to thank the following people who have given of their time, opinions, information, and memories for this book: Richard Basini and Seymour Durst of the Broadway Association; Alex Parker; Jon Starr; Robert Brandt; Gerald Schoenfeld of the Shubert Organization; Dr. Mary Henderson, Wendy Warnken, and Bob Minsky of the Museum of the City of New York; Fred Papert of the Forty-second Street Development Association; Richard Armstrong of Covenant House; Susan Brownmiller and the other volunteers at Women Against Pornography; Robert Rydell and the other lovely employees of the Douglas MacArthur USO Center; and the patrolmen of the Midtown South Precinct and Operation Crossroads. A special thanks to Ruth Schwerin Lowenthal, who gave lovingly of her experience and delightful memories of the 1930s and 1940s in Times Square. My love and gratitude go to Paul, Susan, Floyd, Diane, Jay, Randi, and my agent, Heide Lange, for their unending assistance and support.

Most of the photographs of present-day Times Square were taken by Daniel Meltzer, who lives in New York City. He has recently graduated from New York University. His work has been included in numerous group shows and publications, as well as being the subject of one-man shows. Some of the photographs included in this volume were on exhibit at the Mari Gallery during 1981.

Introduction

Stand long enough on the corner of Broadway and Forty-second Street, the saying goes, and you'll meet everyone you ever knew. Since the first fireworks flashed from the top of the newly constructed Times Tower to usher in the bright new year of 1905, Times Square has played host to billions of guests at a party which has lasted for seventy-five years, with no end in sight. The decorations, refreshments, and dress have changed with the years, as have the entertainments and guests; but to this day, the approach of dusk summons revelers seeking all kinds of pleasures to the brilliant lights of Times Square.

There are other places that rival this glorious intersection of bright lights and surging humanity. However, the Ginza in Tokyo and London's Piccadilly Circus are only offspring of the original and have never quite achieved the glamor, magic, and razzle-dazzle that mean Times Square.

Despite the changing face of the area and the current civic outcry against its moral degeneration, people from all over the world continue to flock there, lured by the enduring mystique of Times Square. Of the countless tourists who have visited New York, can there be one among them who didn't stop to gaze at the bright lights of Times Square?

In 1943 the Broadway Association declared the intersection to be the "most densely populated place in the world at night," claiming that 6,437,814 persons came into the area each week to eat 5,000,000 meals in the restaurants, fill 1,779,408 theater seats, and crowd the dance floors of nightclubs with 225,540 bodies. The numbers continue to soar.

Soldiers and sailors on leave, college students on their first big spree away from campus, flappers, jitterbugging bobby-soxers, dance-hall girls, turn-of-the-century ladies and gentlemen whose wealth afforded them every luxury, bootleggers, horseplayers, theatergoers, Tin Pan Alley hopefuls, star-struck teenagers, visiting dignitaries, tourists from Dubuque to Bangkok, and that special breed known as "street people"—all have come away from the glitter of Broadway and Forty-second Street with their own memories of the party they attended there.

Times Square has become a monument to "good times" in the hearts of the generations of visitors who revisit it time and again through the countless movies, plays, and songs which have been set in and inspired by the unique crossroads. Although many of its landmarks have passed from the scene, they still exist in those memories, as do the names of those who gave the Square its glamorous and colorful reputation.

In the mid-1800s the tiny hamlet of Great Kill, situated on a creek at what is now Forty-second Street, gave way to a group of harness shops, stables, and carriage showrooms in the area just above it, dubbed the Longacre. But with the dawning of the 1890s, the City's entertainment district began to creep slowly up Broadway until an age of architectural, theatrical, and social elegance replaced the shabby remains of Longacre Square. For the social and theatrical aristocracy, Broadway and Forty-second Street soon became *the* place to visit, to dine, to be entertained, and to be seen.

Times Square occupied this position well into the twentieth century, until Prohibition closed the elegant dining palaces and hotels. But soon, enriched by bathtub gin, the underworld took over the empty restaurants, and the era of the speakeasy was ushered in. Such real-life characters as Gyp the Blood, Dago Frank, and Lefty Louie inspired the bootlegging horseplayers of Damon Runyon and brought new color to Times Square.

By 1907 Times Square was aglow with light. Collection of the author

The opening of the first talking movie at the Warner Theater in 1927 marked another important change in the makeup of Times Square. Movie houses slowly pushed the legitimate theaters onto the side streets and took over the more prominent spots along Broadway and Forty-second Street with their flashing marquees. These drastic changes in the ambiance of the Square were little mourned. Indeed, the magicians of Hollywood brought new excitement and life to the capital of entertainment and sent glimpses of that famous intersection to the rest of the world.

It was during Prohibition, the Depression, and World War II that gigantic crowds flooded into Times Square to swoon over their film idols and watch the latest news flash around the Times Tower before wandering off into the fantasy land of amazing creations—the Pepsi Cola waterfalls, Wrigley's fish, and the indestructible man who smoked three packs of Camel cigarettes an hour, filling the Square with fluffy smoke rings. The crowds also gathered for the annual New Year's Eve extravaganzas, begun by Adolph Ochs in 1905; for the election returns, the fight results, the star-studded bond drives, and those joyous moments of celebration on V-J Day.

By day, the intersection of Broadway and Forty-second Street bustles with workers, tourists, and Times Square regulars. Daniel Meltzer

The years following World War II have brought even greater changes to the Square than those of the four previous decades. Now Times Square is a carnival filled with shooting galleries, flea circuses, penny arcades, noisy hawkers, soft-drink stands, souvenir shops, and movie marquees designed to shock, bedazzle, and entice.

Although Times Square has always been a home for burlesque and entertainments of a more "prurient nature," until recently these elements were not considered a serious threat to the area. Today a walk down Forty-second Street and the avenues which cross it, reveals a whole string of movie houses whose marquees proclaim the sexploits of the "Swedish Nymphet" and the "Midnight Plowboy." Peep shows, massage parlors, clubs featuring live nude models, all line the streets of the area. Store windows are filled with magazines with voluptuous models on their covers, dotted with paper pasties large enough to fulfill the requirements of City law but small enough to lure the passerby. Prostitutes of both genders display their wares with considerably less subtlety.

Times Square today is a far cry indeed from the Times Square of the Gay Nineties, but still partygoers by the thousands come each night to take part

Big business in Times Square—New York's unofficial red-light district. Daniel Meltzer

in the festivities there. The camera-carrying tourists in their neat wash-and-wear slacks and dresses, with children at their sides, look conspicuously out of place; but their faces reflect the thrill of being in the entertainment capital of the world. For them, the glamor and excitement are still there.

TIMES SQUARE

In the Beginning There Was Broadway

Although the triangle of Times Square is formed by the intersection of Seventh Avenue, Broadway, and Forty-second Street, Broadway is the major component of the "square." This great street, whose origins precede the arrival of the first permanent settlers in New Amsterdam, has wound its way through the delights of New York northward from the lower tip of Manhattan to the Bronx, through the towns beyond until finally coming to an end in Albany. All that is and was Times Square has been carried along in the wake of this powerful thoroughfare as it has flowed uptown.

Thirteen years before Peter Minuit struck his legendary bargain with the Manahatto Indians, Broadway had played host to its first European tourists—the captain and crew of a Dutch ship named the *Tiger*, which anchored in the Hudson River. When the ship was destroyed by fire, Captain Adrian Block and his men had to spend the winter in four small huts along an old Indian trail, at the site of what is now 45 Broadway, while a new ship was constructed.

With the arrival of Minuit in 1626 and the establishment of Fort Amsterdam at the lower tip of the island, that old Indian trail became a well-trodden street running north from the fort. To the farmers who traveled to the marketplace of the tiny Dutch settlement, it was known as the High Wagon Way. It was Wouter Van Twiller, who succeeded Peter Minuit as governor of New Amsterdam, who officially labeled this trail, along which the Dutch settlers strolled and conducted business, Brede Weg, or Broadway.

Broadway between Park Place and Ann Street, circa 1825. The residence of Mayor Philip Hone is at the far right. New York Public Library Picture Collection

When, in 1664, the British took over the Dutch village and renamed it New York, Broadway remained unchanged. It was this street that pushed beyond the confines of New Amsterdam, moving north as the decades passed and carrying the centers of New York's social and economic life along with it.

The peculiar angles at which Broadway crosses other thoroughfares has always added visual interest to the otherwise static grid pattern of New York City's streets. Each time Broadway connected with another major artery a so-called square would be formed, and each of these would first become an important residential address, then the shopping district with the finest stores, and finally the City's entertainment center. The attraction of Broadway as *the* residential, retail, and theatrical thoroughfare was clear. It was the only street which was well-lit, well-paved, and served by good public transportation. It began at City Hall Common, then pushed north to Union Square at Fourteenth Street, Madison Square at Twenty-third, Herald Square at Thirty-fourth, and Times Square at Forty-second.

After the Revolutionary War, lower Broadway

was the site of many fashionable homes, and the brass nameplates along the avenue identified the residences of George Washington, Alexander Hamilton, and Daniel Webster. The fine shops serving the area included such names as Tiffany, Gorham, and Brentano.

Entertainment in the late eighteenth and early nineteenth centuries centered mostly on the local taverns, where the men socialized; evening diversions for women were few. This situation began to change in the late 1700s when the "pleasure garden," a popular amusement imported from England, attracted City crowds on warm summer evenings. There patrons wandered through vast outdoor gardens, sipped punch or lemonade, and were frequently entertained by singers or small summer-stock theater productions.

The Vauxhall, owned by Joseph Delacroix, opened in 1804 on the site of an old homestead at the corner of Grand and Mulberry streets. It was such a success that, with the financial assistance of John Jacob Astor, Delacroix turned his Vauxhall into the City's largest and most diverse pleasure garden in the area, spanning the distance from

Typical of the early pleasure gardens is this scene at Niblo's. On balconies in the background, patrons dine. New York Public Library Picture Collection

Broadway to the Bowery. Flowerbeds, statuary, shrubbery, rose arbors, and fountains lined the maze of gravel walks that traversed the garden. A small theater opened in one corner and the audience sat in the open air to listen to orchestra music and watch light plays, fireworks, and ballooning exhibitions.

The heart of the growing City, however, was not destined to remain in the original area of settlement. As the second half of the nineteenth century began and as Manhattan became a metropolis, the previously rural life of early New York began to disappear. The City was constantly undergoing change, and it was Broadway that carried the changes northward. The shifting locale of fashionable addresses occasioned New York observer Philip Hone to complain in his diary for 1850, "The mania for converting Broadway into a street of shops is greater than ever. There is scarcely a block in the whole extent of this fine street of which some part is not in a state of change."

Fine hotels and restaurants sprang up along Broadway to cater to resident New Yorkers and to

By 1836 Broadway had developed into a lively thoroughfare. **New York Public Library Picture Collection**

the elegant visitors who came to the City for extended stays. In the opening years of the metropolitan boom, it became impossible for builders to keep up with the growing population, and, as a result, the cost of private housing soared. Middle-class families lived in hotels, since none but the very rich could afford the expense of running a household.

Hunter's, built in 1794 at 69 Broadway, had been the City's first hotel. Soon after the City Hotel opened a few blocks north. Its dining room attracted the social elite, and its ballroom became the scene of important social functions. In 1830 these hotels were eclipsed by the splendor of the Astor House. Built on Broadway and Barclay Street by John Jacob Astor, it was known for the free lunch offered in the bar to the visitors, journalists, and politicians who frequented the hotel.

The early 1850s opened a great hotel era. The St. Nicholas, at Broadway and Broome, with its offerings of elaborate furnishings and evening balls, usurped the elegance of the Astor House. Built at a cost of $1 million, it could accommodate eight

The Astor House, an oasis for journalists and politicians in the 1830s. New York Public Library Picture Collection

The Fifth Avenue Hotel at Twenty-third Street. In 1859, it was considered to be too far uptown to succeed. J. Clarence Davies Collection, Museum of the City of New York

hundred guests and was distinguished by having the first central heating system in New York. The Metropolitan Hotel at Broadway and Prince, which opened in 1852, also provided central heating for its six hundred guests, as well as a "sky parlor," where ladies could sit in the open air and look down upon the fashionable bustle of Broadway.

In 1859 the ultimate luxury hotel opened in a location so far north of the others that it was thought to be suitable only as a summer resort. The Fifth Avenue Hotel at Twenty-second Street and Madison Square offered private baths and a "perpendicular railway"—the first elevator in a New York building.

During the mid-1800s, Broadway bustled with business—carriages, tradesmen's vehicles, sightseers, visitors, and elegant women who promenaded along the avenue and shopped in its stores.

The elevator in Lord & Taylor's, which opened its doors at Broadway and Twentieth Street in 1872. In the late nineteenth century, New York's most elegant shops were on Broadway, and the fashionable shopped along the "Ladies' Mile." **Museum of the City of New York**

The department store of A. T. Stewart at Chambers and Reade streets was the favorite haunt of women whose wealth afforded them the very latest in fashions.

By the 1880s the shops patronized by these fashionable women had consolidated on Broadway in the area between Eighth and Twenty-third streets known as the Ladies' Mile. In the afternoon, Broadway was clogged with the traffic of landaus, broughams, and carriages, while the sidewalks were equally crowded with women dressed in their finest who strolled the avenue and shopped in the stores. The popular establishments of the day included Colonel John Daniell's at the southernmost tip of the mile and Arnold Constable's at Nineteenth Street. Across from Constable's one could find the carpets and furniture in current vogue at W. J. Sloane and Co. New York's social elite were drawn to the second floor of Lord & Taylor at Broadway and Twentieth Street where the exclusive fashions were shown.

Not all of the attractions on Broadway during the nineteenth century were for women. The avenue had a number of concert saloons—watering spots which featured dancing partners for their male patrons, sometimes in addition to singers and boxing

New York City's concert saloons were noted for wild women and entertainment. **New York Public Library Picture Collection**

exhibitions. The Gem at Broadway and Pearl Street was frequented by many of the Tammany bigwigs, and Harry Hill's at Houston Street drew patrons from all social classes.

Other popular entertainments of the era were the elegant gambling establishments of such men as John Morrisey whose "818 Broadway" was the best-known casino in the city. His patrons included such powerful men as August Belmont, Commodore Vanderbilt, and Mayor Fernando Wood. Richard Canfield opened a casino at Twenty-sixth Street and Broadway with the assistance of Diamond Jim Brady. His aristocratic patrons included J. P. Morgan, Henry Frick, Jesse Lewisohn, John W. "Bet-a-Million" Gates, the Whitneys, and the Vanderbilts. When the popular Delmonico's restaurant moved uptown to Forty-fourth Street and Fifth Avenue, Canfield thought it wise to follow his clientele and promptly installed his establishment just two doors away. Frank Farrell's Place, known as the "House with the Bronze Door," was designed by Stanford White and located near the Waldorf Astoria Hotel.

In the nineteenth century the fashionable residential neighborhoods of lower Broadway gradually began to move uptown. Broadway at Astor Place (Eighth Street) was one of the first sites for "socially acceptable" residences, and Union Square (Fourteenth Street) had its day as the home for New Yorkers of wealth and background. The Goelets, Huntingtons, and Roosevelts were among the distinguished residents between Fourteenth and Seventeenth streets. Madison Square (Twenty-third Street) became the center for the nouveaux riches whose fortunes were made in railroad and finance. These tycoons and their families eventually became a part of "the Four Hundred" created by Mrs. Caroline Astor. (It should be noted here that the limit of four hundred socially acceptable families came about because that was the maximum number of guests the ballroom in the Astor home could accommodate.)

As Broadway continued its thrust from the tip of

Niblo's Garden and
Theater in 1828. New
York Public Library
Picture Collection

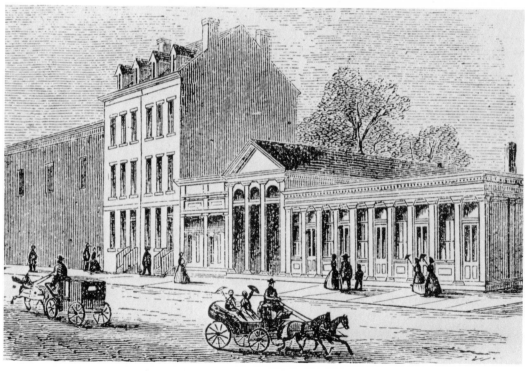

the island into the center of the booming metropolis, the social leaders followed close behind, bringing the businesses that catered to their needs and whims. Next to come were the theaters which provided entertainment for New Yorkers of every social class.

Until the middle of the nineteenth century, entertainment in New York consisted of a few small theaters scattered about Lower Manhattan; because of the slim fare offered, New Yorkers took very little interest in them. What was to become New York's rialto was beginning to take root in the early 1850s around Broadway and Prince Street with Niblo's Garden, a product of the pleasure-garden craze. Here various exhibitions, skits, and productions were staged in an old open-air circus while patrons sat at their tables under the stars drinking beer. William Niblo erected a concert saloon as well as a large theater on the grounds, with the entrance running through the gardens from Broadway. When the popularity of the pleasure garden waned, the Metropolitan Hotel was built on the site, with a lobby entrance into Niblo's Theater. Wallack's Theater, which in 1860 would become the most fashionable of the playhouses in its new home at Union Square, had its beginning at Broadway and Broome Street.

The event that truly stimulated the interest of New Yorkers in the stage and prompted a steady stream of European stars to play before packed audiences in Manhattan was sponsored by none other than P. T. Barnum, the master showman. Barnum had made a name for himself and had helped to increase the growing popularity of Niblo's Garden by sponsoring the appearance there, in 1835, of one Joice Heth, who claimed to be the 161-year-old former nurse of George Washington. Barnum then opened his own American Museum at Broadway and Ann Street in 1842, continuing to draw tourists and New Yorkers alike. It was not until 1850, however, that his name became linked with an important contribution to the New York stage, for it was

Looking south on Broadway in 1850. Barnum's Museum is at the left; the Astor House at the right. New York Public Library Picture Collection

in that year that he brought Jenny Lind from Sweden to perform at Castle Garden.

Never before had a singer of such stature in the European capitals even considered playing on an American stage, but Barnum claimed to have offered Lind more money than any singer had ever received. The publicity surrounding her arrival reached well beyond the boundaries of the City, as did stories of her talent, prestige, generosity, and virtuous nature. She astonished the first-night audience packed into Castle Garden by donating her entire $12,000 share in the opening performance to various philanthropic and cultural institutions in New York. The public adored her, and the furor surrounding her success here encouraged many European singers, actors, and actresses to cross the Atlantic for American tours.

Interest of a slightly different nature surrounded the more colorful figure of Lola Montez. The reputation which preceded her opening in New York was somewhat less virtuous than that of the Swed-

A music title page featuring Jenny Lind, the "Swedish Nightingale." New York Public Library Picture Collection

ish Nightingale, although the theater at which Lola appeared was packed each night with an audience consisting almost exclusively of men.

Montez (born Marie Gilbert in Ireland), after an unsuccessful early marriage, became a dancer who, despite limited talent, was a sensation in Europe because of her beauty and smoldering sex appeal. The royal houses of Europe were scandalized when Ludwig I of Bavaria, who was more than sixty years old at the time, made her his mistress and created her Baroness of Rosenthal and Countess of Lansfeld. The king was eventually forced to abdicate his throne, and Lola fled to England, where she married a second time. She was later charged with big-

*Lola Montez bids
farewell to Europe and
Ludwig I of Bavaria.*
New York Public Library
Picture Collection

amy in London and sought refuge on the Continent, where her problem was conveniently solved when both husbands died a short time later. Lovely, charming, and energetic, she appeared each night before her audiences dressed briefly enough to display even further charms while the male assembly begged for her best-known number, "The Spider Dance." She toured the United States in 1851, appearing at the Bowery Theater in New York. In 1856, after a tour of Australia, she returned to New York to settle there permanently, and caused further sensation by lecturing New York women on the subject of her book, *The Art of Beauty.*

The appearance of Jenny Lind and the resulting string of European celebrities who came to America solidified the interest of New Yorkers in the stage. By 1860, some fifteen major theaters were filled with enthusiastic patrons.

The New York theater began to develop idols of American heritage as well. Edwin Booth leased the

Winter Garden on Broadway, near Bond Street, where all three Booth brothers appeared in *Julius Caesar*. Booth opened his own repertory company, and the innovative realism he brought to Shakespeare and other classic plays brought both success and popularity to the young actor. Unfortunately,

Edwin Booth's portrayal of Cardinal Richelieu. New York Public Library Picture Collection

after his brother, John Wilkes Booth, assassinated President Abraham Lincoln, Edwin was forced into temporary early retirement. But Booth had greatly underestimated the loyalty and respect of his Broadway followers, for when he finally did return to the stage in early 1866, it was to thunderous ovations from audiences who saw no reason to connect his brother's crime to Edwin's talent. A few years later, this support prompted Booth to open his own theater at Sixth Avenue and Twenty-third Street. Although plagued with financial difficulty, the theater was known for its beauty of design and the quality of its performances, and it rivaled the great Wallack's in popularity.

Moving uptown in the 1860s to a new location at Broadway and Thirteenth Street, Lester Wallack's theater became synonomous with quality, elegance, and distinction in both its productions and its audiences. To play at Wallack's assured an actor of almost instant fame; to be seen in the audience on opening night was a requirement of the wealthy and fashionable.

Certainly not all the entertainments offered along Broadway in the 1860s boasted such quality and prestige. The Broadway Theater booked such outlandish productions as *Mazeppa*, a vehicle for the equally outlandish star, Adah Isaacs Menken, who ended the show strapped naked to the back of a horse charging up the theater runway. She shook the solid citizens of New York by bobbing her hair and smoking in public, and quickly became the darling of the Bohemian set.

Having declined steadily over the previous decades, Niblo's Garden returned to popularity with a production which combined dancing, singing, acting, and bare legs. All New York was horrified, but not enough to stop Niblo from reaping enormous profits.

Finally the more respectable theatrical business along Broadway played host to a sensational novelty in the form of "the leg show"—destined to be the ancestor of modern burlesque. The Lydia Thomp-

Lydia Thompson, famed for her touring burlesque troupe, playing Robinson Crusoe, in 1872, with her pet poodle in attendance. Theatre Collection, Museum of the City of New York

son Burlesque Co. opened at Woods' Museum in the fall of 1868 with four stunning and shapely blondes laced into black corsets and sporting flesh-colored silk stockings. These four beauties—prototypes of the showgirl—presented parodies of the customs and manners of the day. Although Lydia's ladies received more feminine patronage than Lola Montez had drawn a little over a decade before, the audience for such entertainments was still principally men.

In the early 1840s a theatrical phenomenon had appeared on the scene and sparked the construction of many new theaters along Broadway. The minstrel show provided energetic escapist entertainment to

The minstrel show—rage of the 1840s. New York Public Library Picture Collection

a citizenry suffering from economic depression in a growing City. Diarist Philip Hone described the period following the financial panic of 1837: "The times are certainly hard. Money is very scarce and provisions are dear . . . yet, with all this, the rage for amusement is unabated." The minstrel show was just what the public needed, and the most popular group, the Christy Minstrels, gained nationwide fame from their home base in Mechanics Hall on Broadway near Grand. The minstrels maintained their popularity for nearly twenty years and the stages of Niblo's Garden, Barnum's American Museum, and the Astor Place Opera House were alive with the music and dance of black-faced performers.

From its roots in Lower Manhattan, the rialto followed the flow of Broadway uptown, first to Union Square, where the Academy of Music held aristocratic sway over the operatic tastes of New York society. The roots of the Academy reached back to the splendor of Astor Place. As a matter of convenience for the socially prominent, private funds were produced from the ranks of the Four Hundred to erect the Astor Place Opera House. From the beginning it was doomed to financial failure. Although the opera house was conveniently located for the Astors, the proprietors failed to take into account the fact that the theater was out of the way for the rest of the City's population. When British actor William Macready, a rival of American actor Edwin Forrest, opened in the 1849 season, a riot broke out between the partisans of each man. The deaths that resulted from the skirmish damned the opera house and it closed shortly thereafter.

The socially prominent simply abandoned the Astor and in 1854 began patronizing the newly built Academy of Music at Union Square. To own a box at the Academy was an imperative for the socially elite, and the rejection of incredible sums of money for a place in this musical society promptly put the nouveaux riches in their crestfallen places.

The newly moneyed businessmen from Wall Street were not the only critics of this monument to old-line aristocracy. Horace Greeley, a popular social critic writing for the *New York Tribune,* advocated burning the building to the ground and said that if the price was not unreasonable, "have it done and send the bill to me."

As the years passed, the anger of those who were judged unacceptable at the Academy prompted a move which was to change the position of opera in the City and to effect the eventual defeat of the old-line elite by the powerful bankers, industrialists, and railroad men, such as J. P. Morgan, William Rockefeller, Jay Gould, and the Vanderbilts, who

The riot in 1849 between the partisans of American actor Edwin Forrest and his British rival, William Macready, spelled the end for the Astor Place Opera House. New York Public Library Picture Collection

assumed leadership of a new social group. Furious at their inability to win the social standing of a box at the Academy of Music, they decided to build their own opera house.

The group hired Josiah Cleaveland Cady to design the new theater on a site at Broadway and Thirty-ninth Street. The exterior of the opera house was hardly imposing, but great attention was lavished on the interior, where the millionaires built for themselves what they had been denied at the Academy of Music. Three tiers of boxes dominated the auditorium; accommodations for less prominent patrons were provided in a balcony above the boxes, a family circle, and orchestra stalls. The first tier of boxes in the house became known as the Diamond Horseshoe; the secondary tier above it had to settle for the appellation Golden Horseshoe.

Monday was the night when society turned out in its finest gems and furs, to the delight of crowds of ordinary New Yorkers who came to gape at the aristocratic finery. The opera was frequently of little importance compared to the show in the glittering Diamond Horseshoe, where the dowagers sat in their boxes wrapped in ermine and sparkling in jeweled tiaras. The management ultimately provided the audience with a diagram that identified all the prominent seat-holders.

While the new opera house was not a financial success, it did achieve the goal of taking attention and patronage away from the Academy. A merger between the two took place and the Metropolitan Opera was formed in 1883.

The Metropolitan Opera House at Broadway and Thirty-ninth Street was built by tycoons whose lack of social standing denied them entry to the prestigious Academy of Music. New York Public Library Picture Collection

Stanford White's Madison Square Garden. Collection of the author

The next jump made by the rialto followed Franconi's Hippodrome uptown to Madison Square at Broadway and Twenty-third Street, where Augustus Saint-Gaudens' lovely but controversial statue *Diana* looked down from the tower of Stanford White's Madison Square Garden. As the first nude female figure to grace a public building, *Diana* shocked some straitlaced New Yorkers, but J. P. Morgan, the principal stockholder of the Garden, held firm, and *Diana* remained despite the protests. The Garden lured New Yorkers into Madison Square with its sports arena, theater, music hall, and a roof garden that later achieved notoriety as the scene of architect Stanford White's murder by Harry K. Thaw.

The Madison Square Theater at Broadway and Twenty-fourth Street was the first theater to use a double stage moved by hydraulic lifts for scene changes, to the constant fascination of its audiences, and an air-cooling system to provide comfort on sultry summer days. The Lyceum at Fourth Avenue and Twenty-third Street drew society audiences like those of Wallack's and, because of its luxurious interior, earned the nickname, "the drawing room of New York theater." It was the first theater in New York City to be lit by electricity.

By the 1880s the length of Broadway between Madison Square and Forty-second Street was firmly established as New York's glittering rialto. With the addition of electric street lamps along this stretch came the name the Great White Way. This mile of Broadway was lined with the most luxurious hotels, and its fashionable bars and restaurants drew visitors from all over the world.

Looking north from Herald Square, 1909. The Byron Collection, Museum of the City of New York

Henry Collins Brown, editor of the popular *Valentine's Magazine*, first voiced what had long been the accepted rule,

All the world came to Broadway to shop, to flirt, to dine, to gamble, to find amusement, to meet acquaintances, and the legend runs that one standing in the portico of the Fifth Avenue Hotel [on the Broadway side] would one day meet any long-sought acquaintance whensoever he might come.

This little legend continued to hold true even after the Fifth Avenue Hotel disappeared from the scene and the proper location for waiting shifted to the corner of Broadway and Forty-second Street.

This miraculous mile boasted such institutions as Daly's, Charles Frohman's Empire, Miner's Fifth Avenue Theater, the Standard, Garrick's, Palmer's,

The Casino Theater at Broadway and Thirty-ninth Street, home of the Floradora Sextette.
Theatre Collection, Museum of the City of New York

and the Weber and Fields Music Hall, featuring such stars as Maurice Barrymore, Fanny Davenport, Robert Hilliard, Otis Skinner, Ethel Barrymore, John Gilbert, Mrs. Fiske, John Drew, and Maude Adams. The last two decades of the nineteenth century truly marked the Golden Age of the theater in New York.

The dawning of the Gay Nineties and the splendid social whirl which accompanied their arrival found a perfect setting in the sparkling glamor of the rialto. On Broadway this was the day of the stage-door Johnny and champagne Charlie, who were distinguished by the number and price of the gifts they lavished on the great professional beauties of the day. The Floradora Girls, Lily Langtry, Sarah Bernhardt, Lillian Russell—these charming and successful beauties set the styles in women's fashions and became popular legends in their day. With their talent for leading fully publicized and colorful "private" lives, they scandalized the public just enough to gain its fascination and admiration.

Nowhere was the fascination of these beauties more evident than at the Casino on Broadway and Thirty-eighth Street. The Casino was designed to provide entertainment in the form of light opera, but it was the charm and shapely curves of the statuesque Casino Girls that filled the theater night after night. It was here that the Floradora Sextette made theatrical history. All six members of the original group were purported to have married millionaires, and they were replaced by others who aspired to the same. Men of great wealth lavished gifts of champagne, flowers, jewelry, and furs upon the Casino Girls just for the privilege of being seen with them in the popular restaurants and clubs of the day. The best known of these beauties received, from the empire-builders of the era, gifts ranging from the usual floral arrangements to country homes.

It was Lily Langtry, the English actress and court favorite, who began this tradition of the pampered beauty. She arrived on these shores with her acting troupe and a shocked America followed her amor-

The interior of the Casino Theater, where marble, gilt, and wicker combined for a sumptuous Victorian effect. Theatre Collection, Museum of the City of New York

The Floradora Sextette in 1900. Theatre Collection, Museum of the City of New York

ous adventures on tour and back to New York, where the infatuated socialite Frederick Beghard installed her in a luxurious Gramercy Park residence.

Another professional beauty was *Miss* Sarah Bernhardt, who, to the delight and shock of the public, was accompanied on her American tour by her young "son." The sensation surrounding the Divine Sarah caused the bustle to disappear from the backside of the metropolitan woman in imitation of Bernhardt's slender, boyish figure.

Lillian Russell, who began her career as a Floradora Girl, most certainly had a talent for the light

*"The Divine Sarah"
Bernhardt, whose beauty
and notoriety caused a
sensation.* New York
Public Library Picture
Collection

opera in which she starred, but her true ability was revealed in her role as a professional beauty. Married three times, she was said to have had romantic liaisons with several wealthy power brokers. Her most famous affair was with industrialist Jessie Lewisohn, who boosted public interest in that relationship by eloping with the mistress of Diamond Jim Brady, a high-living, lavish-spending industrialist who was called King of the Great White Way. Although there was never a real love affair between Miss Russell and Brady, their constant companion-

Lillian Russell, most famous member of the Floradora Sextette, shared the royal throne of Broadway with her friend, Diamond Jim Brady. New York Public Library Picture Collection

ship kept rumors flying—and the spotlight on Miss Russell. When worried about the possible decline of her career because of a serious weight gain (doubtless caused by too many dinners with Brady), Russell took to exercising on the streets of New York on a gold-plated, diamond-studded bicycle provided by Brady.

In many ways, Brady and Russell—the king and queen of Broadway—stand for the glamor and glitter of turn-of-the-century Broadway. Brady, whose fortune from financial speculation and the sale of railroad equipment was rated in excess of $12 million, was known for two great passions. His first true love was for the diamonds he displayed with ostentatious flair. A writer once commented in the *New York Herald* that the diamond stickpin that had become an integral part of Brady's costume "lit up the road ahead of him like the headlight of a locomotive." * It was rumored that his collection included more than twenty-six thousand diamonds.

Dressed and glittering from head to toe—"Them that has 'em, wears 'em," Brady explained—Brady would step out on the Great White Way to give over his attention to the second real devotion of his life —eating. His reputation for ingesting enormous feasts of steak, oysters, and lobster finally occasioned the owner of fashionable Rector's lobster palace to dub Brady "the best twenty-five customers we had." ** Brady described his meals bluntly: "Whenever I sit down to a meal, I always make it a point to leave four inches between my stummick and the edge of the table. And then, when I can feel 'em rubbin' together pretty hard, I know I've had enough." †

And so world interest in the personalities of the rialto grew and continued to blossom each season. The visitors came to walk along Broadway and, in some small way, to be part of its wealth, gaiety, and

---

* Morris Lloyd, *Incredible New York* (New York: Random House, 1951).
** Alexander Kirkland, *Rector's Naughty 90's Cookbook* (New York: Doubleday, 1949).
† Lloyd, *Incredible New York.*

Diamond Jim Brady, "King of the Great White Way." New York Public Library Picture Collection

glamor. They stayed at the Waldorf Astoria on Thirty-fourth Street, paraded along its long marble corridor, known as Peacock Alley. They had drinks at the Hoffman House, took in the shows, and dined at Delmonico's. All the while, they basked in the cosmopolitan light surrounding them and established the Great White Way as a world center of theater and fashion.

What News on the Rialto?

By the time the Gay Nineties were racing to a close, the uptown thrust of Broadway had arrived at Forty-second Street. The glittering entrance it made into that triangle of land could not be rivaled even by Mrs. Astor's diamond-draped appearance on an opening night at the opera. From Madison Square on Twenty-fourth Street to Broadway at Forty-first, the sparkling line of theater marquees and glowing street lamps along the rialto lit up the Great White Way to form an arcade of light through which the adventurous and enterprising marched into Times Square.

What first began as a rolling land of farms and fields surrounding Great Kill, was eventually trans-

The Longacre in 1900. Hammerstein's New York Theater, part of the Olympia complex, is at left. The Byron Collection, Museum of the City of New York

formed into the center for the harness trade to accommodate the transportation needs of the
metropolis growing around it. In 1803, John Jacob
Astor had begun to purchase land in the area of
Great Kill. It was from Astor that William H. Vanderbilt bought a parcel of land for the American
Horse Exchange—now the Winter Garden Theater.
Unofficially named the Longacre after its London
equivalent, in daylight the area was busy with the
buyers and sellers of its trade. But when the horses
were stabled and the doors locked at night, the
Longacre became a gloomy and dangerous section of the city.

A portly little man in a Prince Albert coat, sporting a Van Dyke beard and a long black cigar, was
the first to step out of the bright lights of the Great

*Pioneer of the Longacre,
Oscar Hammerstein I.*
Theatre Collection,
Museum of the City of
New York

White Way into the gloom of the Longacre. No stranger to the New York theater, Oscar Hammerstein I had been an entrepreneur, inventor, and composer for some years before his excursion into the square. Hammerstein the inventor had turned his passion for those long black cigars to his workbench and successfully patented a rolling machine, a cutter, a device which molded twelve cigars at once, a heading machine, and a suction system for spreading and shaping the leaves.

Hammerstein the entrepreneur had opened the Harlem Opera House, the first theater north of Central Park, by the time he was thirty-three years old. In 1892, he opened the Manhattan Opera House on Thirty-fourth Street in partnership with Koster and Bial.

An Orthodox Jew, born in Germany in 1847, Oscar had a quick, scrappy temperament, a love of practical jokes, theatrical tastes which ranged from grand opera to burlesque, and a thoroughly unorthodox view of the theater, business, and life. He once bet $100 that he could write a complete opera in twenty-four hours and then produced *The Kohinoor Diamond* with his own words, music, and money. The production was very expensive and a tremendous flop, but Hammerstein happily collected his money. His offices were to be found at his backstage workbenches. On Tuesday afternoons, he held auditions for amateurs who frequently reduced him to such helpless laughter that he would have to sneak away and leave an assistant to continue the tryouts and pass on the bad news. Sitting backstage on a kitchen chair to watch his own productions, he liked to drop quarters down the dresses of his divas. Sitting out front, he was known to hiss at his own productions, and it was one such hiss that was responsible for his giant step into the gloom of the Longacre that was to be the glitter of Times Square.

George Kessler, a salesman for Moët & Chandon champagne, was a well-known figure on the lobster palace circuit of the Great White Way. Kessler had

taken an interest in a young singer named Marietta
del Dio, whom he tried to convince Hammerstein
to book at the Manhattan Opera House for her
American debut. Hammerstein refused. Greatly en-
amored of the young lady, Kessler went to Hammerstein's partners, Koster and Bial, who agreed to
sponsor the girl at the Opera House.

The night of Marietta's first performance, Kessler
shared a box with Hammerstein. When the crowd
applauded Marietta, Kessler was shocked to see
Hammerstein stand and hiss loudly in full view of
the audience. The two men began fighting on the
promenade outside their box until ushers finally
bounced them onto the street, where they continued their fight before being carted off to the West
Thirtieth Street Police Station. Koster immediately
had Kessler released on bail, but Hammerstein was
forced to wait until a friend came up with the cash.

In court the following morning a judge upheld

Hammerstein's right to hiss a performer in his own theater and dismissed the case. Koster and Bial, with whom Hammerstein had been bickering for some time, paid $370,000 to be finally rid of him.

Oscar sank this money, along with another $2 million, into what he billed as "the grandest amusement temple in the world." The entire block on the eastern side of Broadway between Forty-fourth and Forty-fifth streets was to be the site of his Olympia, which housed three separate theaters: the Lyric, for legitimate drama; the Music Hall, for variety programs; and the Concert Hall for small musical events.

Hammerstein took ads in the *New York Times* to publicize the opening of his theater, describing its

Box seats at Hammerstein's ornate Olympia, which proved to be too large and too costly to operate. Theatre Collection, Museum of the City of New York

imposing "facade of Indiana limestone supported by pillars of polished granite" with "free use of ornamental work . . . yet all in good taste." The interior included a marble foyer with "paintings and statues in every niche" and color schemes in the three theaters of red, blue, and cream combined with gold.

With three separate theaters and the price of tickets ranging from 50 cents to $1.50, Hammerstein was aiming to collect his audience from all social classes, but he was charged by the *Times* of outstripping this goal by selling ten thousand tickets for his six thousand seats on opening night.

By luring such a large number of patrons over the well-defined demarcation line of Forty-second Street, Hammerstein's Olympia was indeed successful in opening up the Longacre as the new rialto for New York. Unfortunately, almost every other aspect of this "grand amusement temple" was, from its opening, a complete failure.

The opening date had to be rescheduled until, finally, on November 25, 1895, the Olympia was ready to throw wide its doors. The following day the *New York Times* reported that carriages, hansoms, and trolley cars began steadily discharging would-be patrons in their finest dress several hours before curtain time. As a cold rain began, the growing mob pushed closer to the doors until, "with the strength of a dozen catapults, they banged at the doors of the new castle of pleasure and sent them flying open." Once inside the theater, the crowds found little comfort. Stairwells were impassable, and ushers stood by helplessly while people fought over seats.

Outside the doors, masses of people still attempted to push out of the rain and into the theater as "puff sleeves wilted and crimped hair became hoydenish in the crush of the rain; toes were trampled . . . trousers were splashed, dresses were torn and still the crowd pushed on."

Extra police assistance divided into two squads in an attempt to shut the "massive carved doors"

but with little success until, finally, at ten o'clock, five thousand soaked, defeated patrons were turned away.

Only twelve hours after the madness of opening night, a pipe joint in the cellar of the theater burst open, sending two workers to their deaths under the drive wheel and hideously scalding others.

Too big to fill and too expensive to operate, Hammerstein's Olympia doomed him to bankruptcy in 1898. In show business jargon it became known, however, as the cornerstone of Times Square—a name justly deserved as the lone pioneer in a territory which would soon achieve world prominence.

The unsinkable Hammerstein did not desert the Times Square he had begun to create. He quickly began to recoup his losses, and in 1899 he opened the Victoria at the corner of Broadway and Forty-second Street which, under the management of Hammerstein's son, Willie, became the vaudeville capital of the world. In 1900 Oscar built the Repub-

Hammerstein's Paradise Roof Garden atop the Victoria Theater. The windmill, cottage, and stream were but a few of its spectacular attractions. New York Public Library Picture Collection

lic just behind it. Bridging the roof of the two buildings was his Paradise Roof Garden. Covered by a glass dome and cooled with streams of water, it attracted thousands of visitors to drink and dance among ponds filled with live swans and a rock grotto inhabited by monkeys.

Despite his visionary insistence upon opening up the Longacre as New York's new rialto, it is doubtful that even Hammerstein could have foreseen the tremendous surge into that small triangle formed at Broadway and Forty-second Street. Theaters, hotels, and sumptuous restaurants quickly followed him over the "northern boundary" and established the Longacre as the new center for metropolitan nightlife.

The theaters of the newly pioneered Longacre, as well as the old standards along the Great White Way, presented astonishing fare in the period between the opening of the twentieth century and the

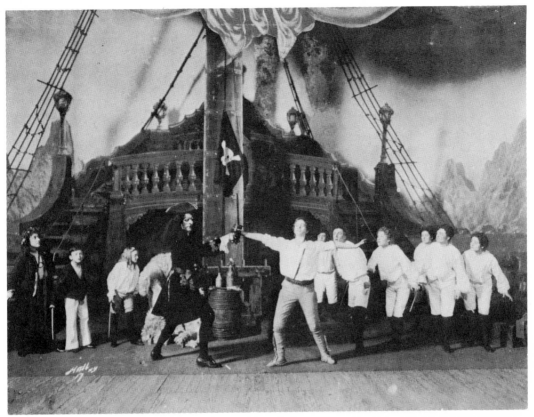

Maude Adams delighted audiences at the Empire in 1905 as Peter Pan.
New York Public Library Picture Collection

advent of World War I. Maude Adams created the eternal Peter Pan and Sarah Bernhardt captured the hearts of New Yorkers with her performance as Camille. In a single season five separate plays by George Bernard Shaw played the stages while that same season entertained audiences with Nazimova in Ibsen's *Hedda Gabler.*

The year 1907 saw the premiere of the *Ziegfeld Follies* and delighted audiences with such musical fare as Lehár's *Merry Widow.* The following seasons there was a change from light musicals to more serious efforts, such as *The Cub*, with Douglas Fairbanks; *Your Humble Servant*, with Otis Skinner; and *The Fortune Hunter,*with John Barrymore.

The theatrical boom was well underway with dozens of houses opening in the years between 1900 and 1920 along Broadway and the side streets west of Times Square. Many of the new theaters lined Forty-second Street which, for a time, threat-

A program cover for the *Floradora girls.* Theatre Collection, Museum of the City of New York

ened the supremacy of Broadway with a myriad of new houses. Oscar Hammerstein's Republic; the New Amsterdam, home of the *Ziegfeld Follies* from 1913 to 1927; the Shubert's Lyric; the Liberty; the American; and the Eltinge (named for the most popular female impersonator of the day) were among the newcomers to establish Forty-second Street in the growing ranks of the rialto.

The scope of entertainment offered in the new theaters of Times Square ranged from variety and vaudeville to legitimate drama and opera. Forty-second Street's American Theater offered lavish spectacles, while the Charles Hopkins on West Forty-ninth Street followed the trend toward smaller, more intimate houses. On West Forty-fourth Street, David Belasco built a theater for his own productions that housed the most sophisticated lighting system of the day. The Astor, on Broadway and Forty-fifth Street, was a feature house for George M. Cohan.

Also built for Cohan's productions was the Gaiety at Broadway and Forty-fourth. Slightly east on Sixth Avenue and Forty-third Street, Thompson and Dundy, builders of Coney Island's Luna Park, erected the mammoth Hippodrome—a five-thousand-seat white elephant which could never support the extravaganzas it was built to house. The Longacre, named for the original establishment of the area, specialized in musical comedies. The Fulton, opened in 1911 on West Forty-sixth Street, was Broadway's first Parisian-style restaurant-theater. The Shuberts opened several theaters during this period of expansion: the Shubert on West Forty-fourth Street—dedicated to the memory of Sam, founder of the dynasty—the Lyric, the Morosco, and the Winter Garden, which marked their entry into musical comedy.

However, the entertainment form which packed the houses of Broadway mingled legitimate talent

The Belasco, built by, and named after, one of the Rialto's most popular producers. New York Public Library Picture Collection

with unsophisticated humor and sensationalism. Singers, dancers, acrobats, comics, and freaks marched across the boards to thunderous applause. As the 1900s drew to a close, vaudeville was gaining

The theatrical boom years of 1900 through 1920 saw the rise of the revue as popular entertainment, and Ziegfeld's Follies came to New York. Theatre Collection, Museum of the City of New York

JARDIN DE PARIS

ATOP THE
NEW YORK
& CRITERION
THEATRES

F. ZIEGFELD JR'S.
REVUE
—
FOLLIES
OF
1908

with BARNEY BERNARD
GERTRUDE VANDERBILT
NORA BAYES
BILLIE REEVES
MAE MURRAY

in popularity. Although viewed with condescension by the legitimate theater, vaudeville giants like Benjamin Keith and Tony Pastor fought to make their bills more appealing to families, and New Yorkers began to flock into the "two-a-day" houses.

Another key factor in the resurgence of the vaudeville stage arose from the competition between the Keith-Albee dynasty and such challengers as Martin Beck, William Morris, and the Shuberts. They all lured the prominent stars of the day with astronomical salaries and wooed the audiences with lavish theaters and star-studded bills.

The Victoria, managed by Oscar's son, Willie Hammerstein, was the most colorful Broadway vaudeville theater. With an instinctive flair for promotion and publicity, Willie packed his theater with audiences who had come to see wrestling champions, murderers, freaks, and women of scandalous reputation, as well as the standard vaudeville fare.

No property seemed too ridiculous for Willie to boost to stardom. Billed as the worst act in America, the Cherry Sisters sang and danced nightly on the Victoria stage behind a net stretched across the proscenium to catch the fruit and vegetables flung from the audience. Moreover, he was not above engineering his own outrageous publicity when an act failed to produce its own. He even arranged for the arrest of one of his performers. The dancer who had been performing the role of Salome boosted the box office receipts after the judge ordered her to wear full tights and appointed a court matron to check her costumes before each performance.

Hammerstein went so far as to feature a return performance of Carmencita—a popular dancer of the Gay Nineties. This was quite a feat for Willie, considering that the dancer had been dead for more than six years.

One performer who came with her own prepackaged publicity was Evelyn Nesbit, the mistress of architect Stanford White, who was murdered by Nesbit's playboy husband, Harry K. Thaw. Just as

*Ahahim's Acrobats—
an act typical of the
fare offered by Willie
Hammerstein at the Roof
Garden of the Victoria
Theater.* Theatre
Collection, Museum of
the City of New York

*Broadway beauty Evelyn
Nesbit was the mistress
of Stanford White, the
wife of Harry K. Thaw,
and a headliner at the
Victoria.* New York
Public Library Picture
Collection

Miss Nesbit was scheduled to open at the Victoria, Thaw, who had been labeled insane and committed to Matawan State Prison, escaped. An armed guard surrounded Miss Nesbit at all times, and she was a topic of conversation for all New Yorkers. Willie's competitors, of course, accused him of arranging Thaw's escape.

Apart from such outrageous fare, the vaudeville stages of the new rialto saw the debuts and performances of such stars as Buster Keaton, Charlie Chaplin, Bill Robinson, W. C. Fields, Marie Dressler, Mae West, Lily Langtry, Will Rogers, Jack Benny, Al Jolson, Sarah Bernhardt, the Marx Brothers, and George M. Cohan.

It was Cohan who made Broadway internationally famous. He, like many other performers of the era, successfully bridged the gap between vaudeville and legitimate theater. And from his studio over Rector's restaurant he wrote the songs that

Rialto favorite George M. Cohan (with cane) and his cohorts in a scene from the Broadway musical, **The Little Millionaire. New York Public Library Picture Collection**

The Hotel Knickerbocker, New York's "country club on Forty-second Street." Museum of the City of New York

paid tribute to the red, white, and blue; mom; apple pie; and the flashing marquees of the Great White Way.

His tireless devotion to solid entertainment most deservedly earned him the bronze tribute which stands on an island in the triangle of Times Square, giving eternal regards to the halls of the rialto.

All of these luminaries—whether of the legitimate stage or of its nouveau riche cousin, vaudeville—spilled from the theaters into the streets, night spots, and restaurants of the Longacre to mingle with the adoring crowds who came each night to see them.

The end of the nineteenth century saw the construction of the Hotel Knickerbocker on what was about to become New York's most famous corner. Referred to as the city's "country club on Forty-second Street," the Knickerbocker sported the world's longest bar—graced by a Maxfield Parrish mural of Old King Cole (which survived the old hotel and now hangs in the bar at the St. Regis Hotel).

Although the bar at the Knickerbocker may have been billed as the city's country club, the truly exclusive social spot was around the corner between Forty-third and Forty-fourth streets. An illuminated green griffin lit the way for Rector's distinguished patronage.

After sending his son George to France to study the art of fine cuisine, Charles Rector closed his Chicago restaurant and, it was rumored, with the backing of Diamond Jim Brady, opened the dining palace on Broadway in 1899 where all elegant New Yorkers went to be seen. The main dining room

The imposing griffin stood guard over Rector's, where Broadway beauties made their entrances. **New York Public Library Picture Collection**

housed the tables of Rector's inner circle, where no ordinary citizen was ever seated. The elite of New York's social, financial, and theatrical worlds waited in line for headwaiter Paul Perret to find a suitably strategic spot for them to rub elbows over fine food and sparkling champagne.

It was at Rector's that "the entrance" was born. Here Broadway beauties waited at the door to be noticed by the orchestra before parading to their seats to the tune of their latest hits. George Rector explained the phenomenon: "While others were forced to pay to see the theatrical stars of the day, the theatrical headliners paid to see Rector's." *

In the same class with Rector's was the lobster palace of Shanley's, just north of Forty-second Street on Broadway. Magnificently appointed by the Astors, who owned the property, Shanley's combined good food, fine wine, and the strains of a small classical orchestra to entertain the stage stars and members of society who, according to *Valentine's Magazine*, "flocked to see the new center of gay life. . . ."

The theater crowd tended to congregate for after-dinner drinks at George Consodine's Metropole Cafe, with the crowd from its restaurant-bar spilling out into the bustle of the southwest corner of Forty-second Street.

By 1904, when the Hotel Astor was built across from the Olympia Theater, the Longacre had been completely transformed. The carriages that had formerly lined the streets waiting for repair now pulled into the square with shining livery to discharge finely dressed passengers before twinkling marquees and lively night spots. The thriving area drew its crowds from all social circles, however, and it became apparent that the boom taking place in the Longacre required a more adequate system of public transportation.

The City had already recognized the need for a rapid transit system to alleviate increasing traffic

* Lloyd, *Incredible New York*.

Built in 1904, the Astor was among the first hotels to offer luxurious lodgings in the Longacre. Collection of the author

difficulties, and in the early years of the twentieth century August Belmont's Interborough Rapid Transit Company began digging up the streets from City Hall, north to Grand Central Station, west across Forty-second Street to Broadway, then north again to 145th Street, to create New York City's first subway line. For five years Broadway looked like one giant excavation site, and the planks which crossed the construction trenches were hardly adequate for the volume of traffic. It became common-place for vehicles to fall into the open trenches.

The chaos in the Longacre's streets during this period was further complicated by additional excavation for a new structure in that triangle of land formed between Broadway and Seventh Avenue. Although it created great havoc for the City's traffic, it was this structure which would finally turn the sights of the City uptown along Broadway and lend to the area its prestigious name.

Publisher Adolph Ochs needed the new rapid transit system to aid in the speedy delivery of his newspapers. He, like Oscar Hammerstein, had the foresight to know that the new boom in trade was moving into midtown Manhattan. After considering a site at the corner of Broadway and Barclay Street across from City Hall (where the Woolworth Building was later erected) and rejecting Park Row as a dying area, he purchased that strange triangle in the middle of the Longacre as the new home for the *New York Times*.

Excavation was completed, the steel framework erected, and on January 18, 1904, the cornerstone of the new Times Tower was laid in place by Ochs's daughter, Iphigenia, who charmingly flubbed her first Broadway appearance by declaring the stone to be "plump [*sic*], level, and square." The Longacre's most prominent landmark would soon be completed.

Previously the buildings that had occupied the triangle—the last of which was the Pabst Hotel—had faced south from the square to accommodate the travelers from the metropolis downtown to the frontier at Forty-second Street. But Ochs did not take one backward glance and established the entrance to his tower on the eastern facade.

The new home for the presses of the newspaper was embedded fifty-five feet below street level, beneath the new subway which would carry the papers to other areas of the City. The home of the *Times*'s offices, however, soared 375 feet into the air to become the City's second tallest building, and

The Times Tower under construction at Broadway and Forty-second Street. Museum of the City of New York

What News on the Rialto? **53**

it was considered by many to be among the City's most beautiful. Referred to as Giotto's Campanile, New York style, the building's architects encased the steel framework in limestone and cream-colored brick and embellished it with carved limestone gingerbread. Upon its completion the Times Tower loomed over the intersections below, and the late afternoon shadow cast by the building stretched the entire length of the square.

Even before the new tower was completed, a campaign was under way to name the subway stop below—and, ultimately, the surrounding area—after its principal edifice. As head of the Interborough Rapid Transit Company, August Belmont had urged that the stops along his subway route be named after some "conspicuous institution" in the area. What more conspicuous institution was there at Broadway and Forty-second than the new Times Tower? He pleaded the case for the name Times Station, and his letters initiated a resolution to the Commission of Streets, Highways and Sewers asking that the triangle of land occupied by the Tower be known as Times Square. On April 19, 1904, the signature of Mayor George McClellan on the resolution made official the name which would soon be known throughout the world.

Hello, Sucker!

The elegant lobster palace society that enjoyed its peak of popularity from the 1890s until World War I was frowned upon in many quarters of New York City. But those New Yorkers who denounced Rector's as a "palace of sin" were soon to long for that stronghold of propriety when, around 1910, cabaret society began replacing the old restaurants as the focal points of Times Square night life.

Live entertainment, drinking, and—worse yet—dancing drew a curious mixture of Broadway society and ordinary citizens into the Cafe de l'Opera on the southeast corner of the intersection at Broadway and Forty-second Street. On the second floor a huge mural depicting the Fall of Babylon symbolized the degeneracy of the undulating dancers below. Here a patron could hear the popular music born of jazz and exemplified by the early songs of Irving Berlin and watch couples who tried to emulate Vernon and Irene Castle, the dancing darlings.

The incredible Murray's Roman Gardens on Forty-second Street had an Egyptian Room where the collection of mirrors, lights, fountains, statuary, tigers, and peacocks were a veritable Hollywood movie setting for the dancers trying out the latest steps on the revolving floor of the cabaret. Weekdays, housewives filled the dance floors, launching a period of prosperity for the gigolos, whose smooth steps and smoother talk earned them expensive wardrobes in exchange for romantic and *dansant* services.

Despite widespread criticism of its steps and costumes, the dance craze struck hard, although employees of the New Amsterdam Theater were

Darlings of the dance, Vernon and Irene Castle, led America onto the dance floor. Wide World Photos

informed that "any member seen Turkey Trotting in a public place will be subject to immediate dismissal."* Apparently, such steps as the Castle Walk, Congo Tango, and the Cake Walk were acceptable to the management. Chicago's Joe Frisco introduced the Jazz Dance at Rector's, and this dance is credited with spawning the "lewd" shimmy, which attracted much attention in those clubs that allowed the patrons to perform it.

A few after-hours clubs still existed for the hardcore drinkers and revelers, and a typical evening on Broadway in 1914 might begin with a round of cock-

* Joe Laurie and Abel Green, *Show Biz from Vaudeville to Video* (New York: Holt, 1951).

Banned on many public dance floors as too suggestive, the Turkey Trot and the Grizzly Bear were nevertheless performed with relish. **New York Public Library Picture Collection**

tails, the theater, some dancing, and, for the truly high fliers, a last call at a fashionable bar. Thus did cabaret society set the style for New York nightlife.

A crushing blow was struck against the alleged sins of the age, however, when, on January 16, 1920, Prohibition became the most hated, debated, and broken law of the land. Doors to the old establishments like Rector's and the new cabarets were boarded without discrimination; the elegant Roman Garden was replaced by Hubert's Flea Circus; and the speakeasy opened its doors to the Roaring Twenties—the decade of society fops, workingmen, theatrical luminaries, prostitutes, politicians, and Wall Street tycoons whose common bond was a search for the liquid gold and a good time.

The growth of the speakeasy moved the nightlife of New York onto dark, quiet side streets, where even the most innocent-appearing residences housed the delights of bootleg liquor and nightly excitement. The speaks ranged from a dark hole in the wall that provided only the liquid sought by its patrons to lavish nightclubs complete with liquor, food, and nightly entertainment. At the bottom of the speakeasy scale were those establishments known as clip joints, where taxi drivers were paid to discharge likely marks in search of booze and broads. Both were plentiful, but at extremely high prices, and many an unsuspecting customer who'd had just a bit too much refreshment found himself signing checks or IOU's for several times the original outrageous amount.

Some of the better-class speaks in midtown operated under the guise of social clubs, and issued membership cards or passwords for entry into the brownstones of the Forties and Fifties. The highest concentration of these clubs was to be found in the West Fifties, where one of the most popular, The 21 Club, is still prestigious.

"Legs" Diamond, owner of the infamous Hotsy Totsy Club, was typical of the generation of nightlife entrepreneurs spawned by the passage of the Volstead Act. New York Public Library Picture Collection

Although the speak was easily the most common establishment serving thirsty New Yorkers (an estimated thirty-two thousand of them cropped up—nearly twice the number of saloons closed by the new law), Times Square housed many lavish nightclubs where patrons could imbibe while enjoying the delights of beautiful show girls, popular entertainers, and the dance crazes of those Roaring Twenties. The Abbey Club on West Forty-fourth Street played host to the elite of a rapidly growing underworld society that frequently held financial interests in such establishments and supplied the products served there. The Hotsy Totsy Club on Broadway, owned in silent partnership by Legs Diamond, was a favorite of young flappers and their flashy escorts. The club made headlines and closed when the "Hotsy Totsy Murders" became the news of the day. In July 1929 a quarrel broke out, ostensibly over the abilities of a prizefighter named Ruby Goldstein. Gunfire was heard, and the police arrived to find two bullet-ridden bodies on the floor of the club. Two of the participants in the argument, one Charlie Green and Legs Diamond himself, had, of course, disappeared. Then, one by one, all the witnesses to the crime were murdered or disappeared. The waiter and bartender were shot; the hatcheck girl and cashier were missing; Diamond's partner, Hymie Cohen, was not to be found; and three other witnesses were killed. With the prosecution unable to produce a single witness, the defendants were acquitted. Such fights were frequent occurrences in these clubs, and the underworld kept the local police, as well as the federal agents, busy.

Perhaps one of the most influential people on the popular nightclub circuit was a woman known as the "Queen of Whoopee"—Texas Guinan, a former showgirl who excelled at giving her eclectic group of customers a good time. She held court in New York's most celebrated nightclubs and formed the basis for cafe society with the mixture of racketeers, Broadway showgirls, artists, intellectuals, and the

social register of the Prohibition years. Having formed a partnership with Larry Fay, a small-time hustler who had social aspirations, Guinan opened the El Fey Club, modeled on the fashionable nightclubs of Paris, then followed with the Three Hundred Club, Texas Guinan's, and the Club Intime.

Frequenting such clubs to keep up with the antics of the newly formed cafe society was a new breed of journalists, exemplified by Walter Winchell, who fed the public curiosity with the vicarious thrills of gossip-turned-news on Broadway. Another man responsible for bringing the exciting flavor of Times Square to the public during those years was Winchell's longtime friend Damon

Former showgirl Guinan and associates show federal agents a bottle that they had overlooked in a raid on the Planet Mars Club. Wide World Photos

Runyon, who, during the Prohibition era, was as big a Broadway celebrity as any theatrical star or producer.

Climbing to the top of his profession early as a reporter-columnist for William Randolph Hearst, Runyon was a frequent patron of Lindy's restaurant, where he began making his contacts with the sporting, gaming, bootlegging, and theatrical personalities of Broadway. These people soon found their way into the short stories Runyon began writing in the early 1930s. Perhaps the best-known work to come from Runyon's characters is the musical, *Guys and Dolls*, which was based on Runyon's short story "The Idyll of Miss Sarah Brown." The main character, Sky Masterson, was modeled after Broadway gambler Titanic Thompson. Masterson is won over by a woman from the Salvation Army preaching the evils of drink and gambling on Broadway. It is in this story that Masterson related the famous advice on "sucker bets" that he got from his father:

Some day, somewhere, a guy is going to come up to you and show you a nice, brand-new deck of cards on which the seal is never broken, and this guy is going to offer you a bet that the jack of spades will jump out of this deck and squirt cider in your ear. But, son, do not bet him, for as sure as you do, you are going to get an ear full of cider.

Runyon, riddled with cancer, continued to hold his respected position in Times Square until his death in 1946. According to the wishes set forth in Runyon's will, Colonel Eddie Rickenbacker spread Runyon's ashes across the Broadway he loved and immortalized. He left one ironic legacy to his life

Damon Runyon, creator of memorable characters modeled on the gamblers and gangsters of Broadway. **New York Public Library Picture Collection**

and times there. A frequent patron of Owney Madden's Club Napoleon, Runyon was also a close friend of the bootlegger whose speak was in the very location that now houses the Damon Runyon Memorial Cancer Fund.

These were the years when the speaks and clubs opened, closed, changed names, and moved with lightning speed. These quick changes were largely brought about by raids from federal agents, one of whom enjoyed a certain popularity with the people he put out of business and became a Broadway character in his own right. Izzy Einstein was generally recognized as Federal Agent Number One as he raided club after club in a variety of hilarious disguises ranging from gravedigger to football player. After gaining entry, Izzy would stroll up to the bar, place his order, and raise his glass to toast the crowd with his familiar "This is a raid!" When he finally retired, Izzy wrote his memoirs, which he thoughtfully dedicated to "the 4,932 citizens" he had arrested.

New York nightlife, characterized by the dazzling nightclub, the shapely cigarette girl, and musical

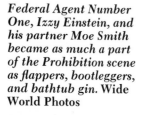

Federal Agent Number One, Izzy Einstein, and his partner Moe Smith became as much a part of the Prohibition scene as flappers, bootleggers, and bathtub gin. Wide World Photos

entertainment was strictly for those who could afford the luxury. Beauty, booze, money, and music flowed freely. Many a career was launched in the better speaks—Beatrice Lillie, Fred Astaire, and Helen Morgan all got their start in the night spots of East- and Westside Manhattan. The Silver Slipper on West Forty-eighth Street, also owned by racketeer Owney Madden, was the home of comedians Clayton, Jackson, and Durante. The Hollywood, on Broadway, was best known for its magnificent chorus line, and Paul Whiteman provided the musical entertainment for Ziegfeld's Midnight Frolic above the New Amsterdam Theater.

During the Prohibition years, the bootlegging kingpins held a firm grasp on the nightlife of Times Square. Their foothold in the territory was an inheritance left by two men who had built a small but powerful gambling empire from a small-time game held in the property room of Willie Hammerstein's Victoria Theater, where the stagehands spent their afternoons and paychecks rolling dice. Numerous Times Square hangers-on wandered in and out of

Roseland—valiant survivor of the great dance era. Patrons from decades past still crowd its dance floor nightly.
Daniel Meltzer

these games, and two of these men came to control the gaming activities in the area that started in that room.

Damon Runyon later wrote about the colorful and basically good-hearted characters who populated the floating crap games in Times Square. But the Sky Mastersons and Nathan Detroits of his stories bore little resemblance to the hard and ruthless personalities of Herman Rosenthal and Arnold Rothstein. The tough games run by Rosenthal and Rothstein were certainly a sharp contrast to the elegant gambling practiced by the socially prominent in the nineteenth century. Appropriately, both Rosenthal and Rothstein were killed on the streets of Times Square.

Herman Rosenthal, one of the real-life gamblers who provided the basis for Damon Runyon's colorful characters. Museum of the City of New York

Police Lieutenant Charles Becker, whose hired gunmen shot Herman Rosenthal to death outside the Metropole Cafe.
Museum of the City of New York

Rosenthal, noted for his big mouth and lack of regard for the established rules of police tribute, refused to cooperate with Lieutenant Charles Becker, who was hungrily attempting to control underworld gambling through "legitimate" police protection. Included in Becker's protection scheme was Rosenthal's establishment on West Forty-fifth Street near Broadway.

After suffering the policeman's threats and thwarting attempts by killers hired to gun him down, Rosenthal countered by threatening to expose Becker to the newspapers. At Becker's direction four gunmen were hired by Big Jack Zelig, an infamous protection agent. The four finally caught up with Rosenthal outside the Metropole Cafe, where the bullets of Gyp the Blood, Dago Frank, Lefty Louie, and Whitey Lewis ended Rosenthal's rule over Times Square's illegal gambling.

Rothstein, whose activities extended well beyond his gambling interests on West Forty-fifth Street, was also known as the "banker for racketeers." He had considerable real estate investments, personal wealth, and power. Known as a cool but deadly gambler, Rothstein was suspected of being involved in the fixing of the 1919 World Series, but was never formally charged with the crime. But in 1928 Rothstein's sharp business instincts began to fail. He soon found himself in the uncomfortable position of owing over $300,000 to the participants of a card game hosted by fellow racketeer George McManus. Foolishly, Rothstein tore up the IOU's and questioned the honesty of the game. McManus, upon whom the responsibility fell, phoned Rothstein at Lindy's, his favorite hangout, and summoned him to a room at the Park Central Hotel. The elevator operator discovered the fatally wounded Rothstein near the servants' entrance on Fifty-sixth Street.

Those who followed Rosenthal and Rothstein into Times Square extended the range of illegal activities there from gambling to extortion, prostitution, and numbers. Lucky Luciano founded a lucrative trade in organized prostitution, operating from the City's speakeasies and nightclubs. Rothstein's protégé, "Dandy Phil" Kastel, joined forces with Frank Costello in distributing to speaks and candy stores the slot machines Mayor Fiorello LaGuardia was so fond of smashing.

Ultimately, these men moved into legitimate enterprises with money and contacts made largely from illegitimate activities. Bill Dwyer was a longshoreman who became wealthy in the rum-running syndicate; he opened an office in Times Square to direct his racetrack, as well as several of the area's nightclubs in which he had partnerships. A small-time hood named Waxey Gordon finished a prison term before he, too, opened a suite of offices on the corner of Broadway and Forty-second Street. The backer of several successful Broadway musicals, Gordon also owned and operated two hotels just west of Times Square.

The man responsible for keeping all these businesses running smoothly and for defending their owners in court was a criminal lawyer named William J. Fallon, whose colorful life was the subject of a book, *The Great Mouthpiece,* by Gene Fowler. Fallon quickly gained a reputation to rival Diamond Jim Brady's as a Broadway playboy. With a new chorus girl on his arm each night, he appeared in every popular Times Square night spot but was most frequently found with the social set at Texas Guinan's.

The times were hot and excitement ran high during Prohibition. The open rebellion against the despised Volstead Act, which outlawed the manufacture and sale of alcoholic beverages, led to wild partying and New York's nightlife was one continual celebration. The decade saw the rise of the popular tunes from Tin Pan Alley, the Egyptian "craze," generated by the discovery of King Tut's tomb, the birth of the crossword puzzle, and the debut of the talking movie. On everyone's lips were the names of Irving Berlin, Charles Lindbergh, Bobby Jones, Jack Dempsey, and Babe Ruth. An entire nation was doing the Charleston.

In the boom years of the 1920s the growth of theaters continued in Times Square. While movie theaters were opening along the avenues, the side streets were now lined with the marquees of fine legitimate houses. The decade saw the erection of Irving Berlin's Music Box, the St. James, the Ambassador, the National, and the Biltmore.

Broadway remained the official rialto, as its challenger, Forty-second Street, saw only two new theaters, the Times Square and the Apollo, join the ranks of those built earlier in the decade, many of which had already been converted to vaudeville,

The Charleston, dance craze of Prohibition nightlife. Wide World Photos

burlesque, or movie houses. Sporting the names of some theatrical greats of the era were the new marquees of the Ethel Barrymore, Earl Carroll's Theater, Hammerstein's, the Martin Beck, Jolson's, the Forrest, and the Ziegfeld.

Opening nights of the era gave theatergoers *Funny Face* (at the Alvin), *Rio Rita* (the Ziegfeld), *Caesar and Cleopatra* (the Guild), Jolson's *Bimbo* and *Madame Pompadour* (the Martin Beck). Most theatrical entertainment in the Roaring Twenties followed the lead of cafe society, and both the Broadway stage and the Hollywood set began to spice up their fare with the sexual overtones. The *Demi-Virgin, Abie's Irish Rose, Charlie's Aunt, A Bill of Divorcement, The Circle,* Mae West's *Diamond Lil, Desire Under the Elms,* and *Strange In-*

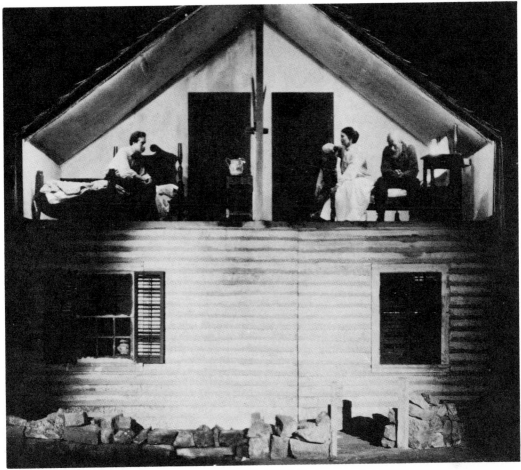

The 1924 theater season included such fare as Eugene O'Neill's *Desire Under the Elms, with Walter Houston.* New York Public Library Picture Collection

terlude were all Broadway stage productions of the decade. Revues in the style of the *Ziegfeld Follies*, with their shapely chorus lines, gained in popularity on both the stage and nightclub circuit. Mae West drove audiences wild performing the shimmy onstage in *Mimic World.*

It was the dancing public, however, that made the greatest mark. The Charleston was replaced in 1926 by the Black Bottom, and public dance halls like Roseland and the Tango Palace—home of the ten-cent dance—quickly opened their doors along Broadway to enormous profits. Times Square, like the rest of the nation, was on its feet and dancing.

The revelry came to an abrupt halt on October 30, 1929, when *Variety* carried the headline: WALL STREET LAYS AN EGG. The booming economy that

provided the cash needed for New York's high-living nightlife crumbled, and the Roaring Twenties quickly gave way to the Great Depression.

The 1930s were marked by disappointment and disillusionment. Just as Prohibition closed the doors of Times Square's greatest landmarks—later replaced by new ones—so the Great Depression took its toll on the glorious nightlife of Broadway.

Vaudeville, unable to keep pace with the high times of the Twenties, had been moribund for some time, but the final blow came in 1930. It was announced that the Palace would close for alteration—to be reopened as a movie house. Theater owners could no longer afford the salaries commanded by big-name acts, and vaudeville houses across the country quickly followed the Palace's lead.

Legitimate theater also suffered. Middle-class patrons could no longer afford theater tickets, even though the theaters featured plays starring some of the greatest names of the time. The Depression had hit actors as well as everyone else, and directors were able to choose from a host of talent. Since half its active members were unemployed, Actors Equity did not recruit new members. By 1931, 45 percent of Broadway's theaters were dark. By the summer of 1932, only six shows were playing on Broadway.

The frivolity of the 1920s gave way to a serious, if not grim, tone in the thirties. Reading became the most popular national pastime, with listening to the radio running a close second. It was not until the election of Franklin D. Roosevelt in 1933 and the introduction of his New Deal policies that the economy began to slowly recover, with Broadway theaters and nightclubs reflecting the turn in the national economy and morale.

In 1933, however, a joyful crowd poured into Times Square to celebrate the repeal of the Volstead Act. Repeal threw open the dark entrances of the speakeasies, many of which converted to legitimate nightclubs dedicated to exclusivity to heighten their appeal. Nothing made the public

Unloading legal beer at a Broadway club, 1933. Wide World Photos

want to get into a club more than the word that its membership and reservations were limited.

The New York stage also began to recover in the mid-1930s, and playgoers were delighted by John Gielgud's portrayal of the unhappy prince in *Hamlet*; George M. Cohan's *I'd Rather Be Right*; George S. Kaufman and Moss Hart's *You Can't Take It with You*; Thornton Wilder's *Our Town*; John Steinbeck's *Of Mice and Men*; William Saroyan's *The Time of Your Life*; Lillian Hellman's *The Little Foxes*; Philip Barry's *The Philadelphia Story*; Moss Hart and George S. Kaufman's *The Man Who Came to Dinner*; Elmer Rice's *Street Scene*; and Clarence Day's *Life with Father*, to name only a few of the remarkable productions presented from 1934 to the end of the decade.

In 1936 the first Big Band swing contest, featuring Louis Armstrong, Red Nova, Artie Shaw, and Paul

Shubert Alley in the 1930s, as Broadway begins a recovery. The legend reads: "In honor of all those who glorify the theatre and who use this short thoroughfare." **New York Public Library Picture Collection**

Whiteman, was held in the Imperial Theater, and in 1937, Benny Goodman's opening at the Paramount brought six thousand young fans screaming into Times Square. By 1938, the Big Bands were blossoming into the craze that would mark the 1940s. Jitterbugging fans jammed the Paramount, Roxy, Loew's State, and the Strand to swing with the music of their favorite bands and musicians— Kay Kyser, Tommy and Jimmy Dorsey, Eddy Duchin, Guy Lombardo, Count Basie, Benny Goodman, and Fats Waller. A novel item called the jukebox took swing to teenagers across the country.

Nightclubs also turned to the music of the day, booking bands, crooners, and female vocalists. New hot spots were the Rainbow Room on top of the RCA Building, with its revolving dance floor; Billy Rose's Casino de Paree on West Fifty-fourth Street,

The Turkey Trot and Charleston give way to Jitterbugging as the hot sound of swing sweeps Broadway. New York Public Library Picture Collection

Glenn Miller, one of the brightest stars in the Big Band galaxy. New York Public Library Picture Collection

where fans could dance in the spotlight on a raised stage in front of the band; the Palais Royal, where the music of Morton Downey pulled in huge crowds, opened in Hammerstein's former Manhattan Casino theater. Even Child's Restaurant in the lobby of the Paramount Building installed a swing band.

Things French came into vogue in the middle thirties; West Fifty-second Street flourished with bistros, and the more risqué entertainments associated with Paris found patronage in New York nightlife. Typical of the entertainment in these *boîtes* was Sally Rand's fan dance. Rand became the drawing card for the Paradise at Broadway and Forty-ninth, which was known for its blonde, blue-eyed chorus line. The International Casino opened across from the Hotel Astor; its popular prices drew massive crowds, which began to hamper the trade of the more "exclusive" and established nightspots. Another middle-priced spot was the Hollywood, a "family" club where dinner and a two-hour show cost $5.00. Jack Dempsey's Broadway bar drew the sports crowd, and Billy Rose's Diamond Horseshoe flourished. Rose's Casa Manana was a lavish club that capitalized on the chic Latin theme of the day. It replaced the defunct Earl Carroll's *Vanities*, which had advertised "Through these portals pass the most beautiful girls in the world." Rose tried to follow the tradition.

Popular with theatergoers ever since its opening in 1921 is the Times Square institution—Sardi's. An opening night on Broadway is still followed by the traditional party at Club Sardi, where anxious stars, directors, and producers await the reviews.

Another Times Square institution for over forty years was Lindy's, known throughout the world for its cheesecake. More than just a luxurious Broadway delicatessen and family dining spot, it was the gathering place for newspapermen such as Walter Winchell, Damon Runyon, and Leonard Lyons, and other Broadway personalities and racetrack habitués. Here they exchanged local gossip and friendly

Billy Rose inspects the candidates for the chorus line at his glittering Diamond Horseshoe.
New York Public Library Picture Collection

insults with the waiters, whose acerbic comments added much to the character and vitality of the place. When Lindy's closed in 1969 after its sale to Longchamps, restaurateur Toots Shor remarked, "It's a shame to see a place like this turned into a whatsiz."

Some critics date the decline of Times Square to the Great Depression, when the area began to direct its appeal to the average New Yorker, turning away from the exclusivity of the Rector's era and the nightclubs of the twenties. Although there were still lavish night spots in Times Square in the 1930s, there can be no question that the empty spaces created by the economic depression were quickly filled by popular entertainment, changing the character of the Square. Many of the legitimate theaters, darkened by bankruptcy, were converted into movie houses, and the carnival atmosphere which has come to stand for Forty-second Street had begun a decade earlier with the opening of Hubert's Flea Circus on the site of Murray's Roman Gardens. Featuring the standard sideshow attractions (the bearded lady, dancing midgets, the human skeleton, and the wild man from Borneo) Hubert's was among the first to bring an air of Coney Island into Times Square. Penny arcades and similar amusements quickly followed.

Burlesque was another form of entertainment that changed the atmosphere of the Square. The burlesque shows at the Casino and other such theaters in the Gay Nineties were considered daring for

The striptease—a taste of things to come for the Times Square area. **New York Public Library Picture Collection**

their day, but they were still a far cry from the frank fare of the thirties. With little to offer but nudity, the stripteaser did her standard routine while walking down the runway. A comedian filled in the gaps between performances. With headliners like Gypsy Rose Lee, burlesque quickly became one of the most popular entertainments in the country for blue-collar men. Although glamorized in such Broadway musicals and Hollywood films as *Gypsy*, *Zip*, and *The Night They Raided Minsky's*, the raucous, frequently inebriated male audience of the burlies further cheapened the Square.

The Minsky family, undisputed royalty on the burlesque circuit, moved their productions into Times Square by purchasing the Central Theater from the Shuberts in 1931. One by one the theaters which previously booked legitimate fare fell to the lure of burlesque, vaudeville, and the movies. The Gaiety and Apollo theaters were two that fell to burlesque for their survival before joining the Globe, Cohan's, the Astor, and the Broadway in converting to motion pictures. The Winter Garden fell to the "talkies" for a brief period in the early Depression years.

Despite its decline in certain areas, Times Square still maintained the glamorous image provided by society nightlife and continued to draw crowds of out-of-towners to the flash and dazzle. The pace had quickened some since the elegance at the turn of the century, and it probably would have been difficult for Diamond Jim Brady to recognize his Broadway in the center of jitterbuggers and cafe society; but the magnetic attraction remained.

The Movies Come to Town

Three sailors on leave in New York City wander the streets gawking at the buildings, lights, traffic, and beautiful girls. Awestruck in unfamiliar territory, two of them turn to their Brooklyn-born buddy whose guidance comes with musical accompaniment.

The sailors, bearing striking resemblances to Frank Sinatra, Gene Kelly, and Jules Munshin, sing and dance across the backdrop of Times Square—

Three sailors on leave participate in one of the world's favorite sports, as On the Town *brings New York—and Times Square—to the nation.* **Movie Star News**

the streets filled with bright lights, people, and excitement. Despite the jaded reputation of New Yorkers, only on the silver screen could three sailors carry on like this without attracting a glance from the crowd in Times Square.

The full-blown arrival of the movies in Times Square is an integral part of the appeal of the Square, although to many it also represents its decline. There are those who maintain that movie marquees gaudily announcing the likes of *The Fiend from Outer Space* brought people to Times Square who were not regular theatergoers.

It is certainly true that the legitimate theaters were slowly crowded into the narrow confines of the cross streets while Broadway and Forty-second Street succumbed to the increasing popularity and profit of the movie houses. But, simultaneously, the

Times Square "grinders" lure the passing crowd into the movie house. **New York Public Library Picture Collection**

movie houses in such places as Springfield, Ohio; Topeka, Kansas; Helena, Montana; and Athens, Georgia, attracted audiences whose first, and sometimes only, experience with the thrill of Times Square came from such films as *On the Town, Forty-second Street,* and *Broadway Melody.* These films glorified the crossroads and intensified the glamorous lure of the Great White Way.

Movie mogul Adolph Zukor bragged publicly, "Show me any other industry that has done so much for Broadway." In the sense that the films attracted countless crowds to the Square, created new business, and brought the thrill of Broadway to middle America, he was right. But the theaters whose marquees once bore such names as Maude Adams, Otis Skinner, John Gilbert, and Helen Hayes may have cursed his words in their new quarters away from the main thoroughfares of Times Square.

Certainly the theaters that adopted the infant kinetoscope, the first moving pictures patented by Edison in 1891, and began running the popular reels as an additional attraction must have regretted taking in such a spiteful child when, after long years of painful decline, the Broadway curtain rang down on the last vaudeville performance at Loew's State Theater in 1947.

The "poor man's amusement" had originally attracted a new audience that rarely attended the legitimate theater. Family groups began filing into the nickelodeon houses in 1899 to watch chase scenes, hurled pies, and newsreels. But the storefronts and makeshift theaters where these films were showing were quickly outgrown by the crowds they attracted. Catching on to the trend, the small-time vaudeville houses of the day became the foster homes of the infant industry. Hammerstein's entered the business by showing the Gans-Nelson fight of 1908 with the added attraction of a live referee to interpret the bout. The Cameraphone, a step into the unexplored territory of talking films by means of phonograph records, was introduced at Hammerstein's Roof Garden. Camer-

Edison's Projectoscope

9th and Pacific Ave.

The Wonder of the Age!

Will be exhibited some of the most WONDERFUL MOVING SCENES ever shown by a Projecting Machine

PROGRAM FOR THIS WEEK:

1. TURKISH SOLDIERS. 10000 Turks Marching to Battle.
2. CARD GAME. 3 Frenchmen playing cards—Very Funny.
3. CAVALRY CHARGE The French Cavalry charging at full speed.
4. SNOW BALLING. This is a very realistic and amusing scene.
5. N. Y. Fire Patrol Entire company running at full speed to a fire on Bleeker street.
6. BURNING STABLE. Very startling.
7. RESCUING HORSES and WAGONS FROM THE STABLE.
8. RESCUE. Firemen taking people through the flames.
9. THOS. A. EDISON. The great inventor at work in his chemical laboratory.
10. FARM YARD. Little girl feeding chickens and ducks.
11. LOVE IN THE PARK. Dude makes a mash— mama appears.
12. MAY IRWIN and JOHN RICE.
13. OLD PIER. Waves dashing over the old pier — Bar Harbor.
14. ANNA BELLE. The famous French dancer
15. Black Diamond Express Fastest train in the world.
16. Arrival Train arrives at a station in the Lehigh Valley R. R.
17. Buffalo Horse Market Showing the finest horses in N.Y. State.
18. Hurdle Jumping Soldiers jumping their horses over hurdles.
19. Irish Politics. Very Amusing.
20. Water Melon Contest. 2 colored men eating melon for a prize.

Dont fail to see the Projectoscope.

Doors open at 1 p m to 5 p m and 7 p m to 10 p m. for Ladies, Gentlemen and Children.

CHANGE OF SCENES WEEKLY.

Admission - - - - 10c.

War Scenes positively next Saturday. A breakdown at the Edison factory has delayed them a few days,

aphone, like other poorly synchronized attempts at combining sound with film, was a disastrous flop.

Some penny-wise vaudeville houses attempted to keep audiences from exiting to beat the rush during the last act by showing an inexpensive film. Little did the owners realize that their money-saving solution would quickly put vaudeville in the red, for the novelty of film itself quickly wore off, and increasingly sophisticated fans began to seek out such screen personalities as Charlie Chaplin, Theda Bara, and Mary Pickford. Broadway stars began to trickle westward, lured by the salaries bestowed on film favorites. Ethel Barrymore received $10,000 for a film version of *Captain Jinks of the Horse Marines* and was quickly followed by Weber and Fields, Will Rogers, Eva Tanguay, George M. Cohan, Billie Burke, John Barrymore, and even the great Enrico Caruso. Vaudeville booking giants like Albee's were helpless to stem this tide because of the phenomenal salaries and rising quality of the motion pictures.

As the quality and sophistication of the films increased, so did the houses they were shown in. Laws regarding sanitation, ventilation, and fire prevention were passed. Thus all elements combined to give birth to a new phenomenon—the movie palace. In 1914 the Strand at Broadway and Forty-seventh Street introduced New York to the first theater designed exclusively for the movies. Built at a cost of $1 million, the theater had a live thirty-piece orchestra and an organist. Its three thousand seats were filled at the opening, which featured *The Spoilers* for 25 cents. In the same year that portion of Hammerstein's beloved Olympia, previously known as the Lyric, became the Criterion and was purchased by Vitagraph Studios. Broadway was aglow with its $10,000-electric sign.

Important actors and luxurious theaters led to higher-quality feature films that filled the movie houses and brought greater profits. In 1915, *Birth of a Nation* opened at the Liberty Theater, converted from a legitimate theater, with a huge adver-

The lobby of the Strand Theater, one of New York's most opulent movie palaces. Theatre Collection, Museum of the City of New York

tising campaign which helped make Broadway history as the film packed the house for forty-four straight weeks. By 1919 it was clear that the movies were surpassing all other forms of entertainment.

The Hollywood moguls not only lured Broadway stars to California, but quickly followed up the successful stage productions with film versions of the plays. Broadway was astounded when Hollywood producers snatched up the rights to *Within the Law* for the incredible sum of $100,000. *Birds of Paradise* also went for $100,000, and *Romance* for $200,000. The high prices for film rights led to some dreadful fare, as Broadway producers put on a few true disasters designed only for a quick sale to Hollywood.

The Roaring Twenties saw an ironic twist in the relationship between the new movie industry and vaudeville, its original sponsor. Thirty-five thousand patrons filed into movie theaters at least once a week. The infant industry had quickly outgrown its parent. Vaudeville found itself second on the bill, bowing to feature films in the starring role. Marcus Loew, head of the nation's largest small-time vaudeville chain, purchased the property at Broadway and Forty-fifth Street previously occupied by the Bartholdi Inn. Here he opened the Loew's State Theater, where live acts were coupled with films in an attempt to bolster box-office bombs. (Loew created a furor among theater owners when he purchased Metro films and put his name on the movies. Rival theater owners showing the films protested advertising the name of the theater next door.)

Period films and costume spectaculars came into vogue in the early 1920s with such features as *Robin Hood, Ben Hur,* and *The Four Horsemen of the Apocalypse.* The dashing heroes of these films quickly became the matinee idols of the day, and women flocked to see Douglas Fairbanks, Ramon Novarro, and Rudolph Valentino. When Valentino died in New York in 1926, a crowd of thousands lined up over a stretch of eleven blocks to see him

The casket of silent-screen idol Rudolph Valentino is carried into St. Malachy's. Thousands of fans lined Broadway, but were kept away from the area of the church during the funeral services. **Wide World Photos**

as he lay in state at a Broadway funeral home. Police were hard pressed to control the emotional outbursts that spread among Valentino's followers.

The film industry quickly took the lead in building luxurious and splendid theaters. In 1926 the lavish Paramount opened to a record first-week box office of $80,000. Police patrols were necessary to control the crowds that came to see the new movie palace. But the house that surpassed all others in luxury, comfort, and elegance, opened at Fiftieth Street in 1927. The Roxy cost $8 million to construct, had seats for more than six thousand custom-

The glowing marquee of the Paramount lit Broadway for New York moviegoers. Collection of the author

Called the "Cathedral of Motion Pictures," the Roxy had seats for more than six thousand customers. Collection of the author

ers, and provided a symphony orchestra, in addition to a spectacular stage show and film. The audience wound around the block waiting to buy tickets for the opening of *Wolf's Clothing*, a second-rate film, at the astronomical price of one dollar. Of course, the customers weren't paying to see a film but to be inside the ultimate New York movie palace. The term *Roxy service* quickly became synonomous with elegance and luxury.

The movie palaces were frequent settings for another entertainment phenomenon—the premiere. Arc lights flooded Times Square with even more brilliant light than usual, and fans pushed through the Square to jockey for a position from which to see the fantastic array of Hollywood stars arriving in limousines for the New York premiere of their latest films. Teenagers jumped and screamed, flash bulbs popped, and police held back the adoring crowds as Clark Gable, Joan Crawford, Vivien Leigh, Cary Grant, Lionel Barrymore, or Marlene Dietrich smiled, waved, and posed for pictures before entering the theater.

Vaudeville continued to supplement the movies.

Such great two-a-day entertainers as W. C. Fields, Eddie Cantor, Joe E. Brown, Ed Wynn, and George Jessel went to Hollywood to make films. And then Al Jolson, on his second trip to Hollywood, made a tremendous breakthrough. Jolson's first film attempt had ended disastrously when he discovered

that he couldn't carry the required love scenes without his trademark blackface and clowning. He walked away from the unfinished film fiasco and returned to his success on the stage. But in the mid-twenties Warner Brothers was able to lure Jolson west again with the promise of an opportunity to perform in his makeup and actually sing in the film. Movie history was made when the first successful feature-length talking film, *The Jazz Singer,* opened on October 6, 1927.

Vaudeville had lost its best to Hollywood, and the growing film industry soon overtook its predecessor in popularity. The process began after World War I. In 1919 the vaudeville stage was divided into two highly competitive camps, with a great deal of internecine squabbling. Keith-Orpheum, the major circuit, sought an upper-class audience for its vaudeville citadel, the Palace on Broadway. The smaller circuits, like that of Marcus Loew, drew a local family crowd at low prices.

The small-time circuits were the first to succumb to the appeal of films, combining movies with vaudeville shows. By 1920 the box-office draw of vaudeville had begun to weaken, and a quarter of the houses offering vaudeville-motion picture combinations switched to films exclusively.

The Orpheum tried offering four-a-day shows at reduced prices, and by 1926 four-a-day had become continuous performances in the twelve remaining big-time vaudeville theaters in the country. By then 96 percent of the theaters in the United States were featuring motion pictures, with vaudeville, burlesque, and legitimate theater accounting for the remaining 4 percent.

There could be no doubt that film had surpassed vaudeville in value, entertainment, and even the luxuriousness of its theaters. High-priced live acts just could not compete with thirty performances a week at admissions ranging from fifty cents to one dollar. The vaudeville circuits grew desperate and began offering, too late, stage shows and big-name bands; the Palace went so far as to place an electric

The Palace offered some of the biggest names in vaudeville in 1932. Theatre Collection, Museum of the City of New York

piano in the lobby. The names on the marquees in those last days of vaudeville were some of the greatest that ever appeared: Fred Allen, Kate Smith, Harry Lauder, Mae West, Eva Tanguay, Rudy Vallee, the team of Clayton, Jackson and Durante, and the up-and-coming swing bands like Paul Whiteman's (with Ruth Etting) and Fred Waring's Pennsylvanians. It was to little avail; as 1927 drew to a close, the Palace was the only big-time vaudeville theater left in New York.

During the shaky Depression years the legitimate Broadway stage became a luxury few could afford.

Hollywood also faltered. The talking movie was far from perfected, but it did drive out such early stars of the silent screen as John Gilbert and Ramon Novarro. Even Mary Pickford announced her retirement.

Hollywood's problems brought a brief reprieve to vaudeville activity, as the Paramount and Strand were forced to strengthen their motion-picture bills with name acts, entering into competition with the Palace for headliners. By 1933, however, all hope

A 1929 program from the Palace—undisputed capital of vaudeville entertainment. **New York Public Library Picture Collection**

was lost when Hollywood solved the sound problems. Broadway gasped when the Palace announced the completion of a sound-wiring system and opened as a film house with the former two-a-day headliner Eddie Cantor starring in *The Kid from Spain*. The Paramount, Strand, and Roxy continued to bolster their box office with big-name bands.

The economic pressures of the 1930s left vaudeville stages empty, and some of Broadway's finest legitimate houses closed. Ready to step into the empty, darkened houses, the movie industry took over those theaters, providing the necessary escape fare for the average citizen. The Astor, Bijou, Broadway, Central, Empire, Cohan, Harris, Lyric, New Amsterdam, Criterion, Selwyn, Times Square, and Ziegfeld all became motion picture theaters. Even Willie Hammerstein's Victoria was gutted by "Roxy" Rothafel and converted into the Rialto movie theater. The age of celluloid had arrived in Times Square. Along Forty-second Street, where elegant theaters once featured live performances by the nation's leading actors and actresses, movie houses began to flourish.

Today the once-new and modern movie houses, featuring major first-run motion pictures, offer, for the most part, a mix of adventure films, reruns, and out-and-out pornography. The responsiblity for the decay along Forty-second Street has fallen on the shoulders of the theater owners who converted the legitimate theaters to motion picture houses. It has yet to be proved, however, whether the motion pictures actually pushed out the legitimate theaters or whether they saved the physical structures that were doomed because of a sagging market. But the fact remains that the movie palaces like the Roxy and the Paramount, built along Broadway and Seventh Avenue, dwarfed the Forty-second Street houses in size and elegance. Unable to compete with the splendor of these new theaters, the older houses began lengthening their hours until they became all-night grinders that depended on male-oriented second-run or older films, emphasizing violence and action. The whole tone of Forty-second Street quickly changed from elegance and formality to a honky-tonk and carnival atmosphere, alive with suggestive advertising and garish marquees. One theater even added an electric chair to the bizarre displays lining what had become known as "the Strip."

When the motion picture was firmly established as the single most important entertainment form in the nation in the late twenties and early thirties, Hollywood began to restore some of the romance it had taken from Broadway's fabulous rialto. Americans who had never set foot in New York came to know the City and, more specifically, Times Square as intimately as their hometowns when the films began to portray the most exciting, glamorous, and lively setting of all—the Great White Way.

The screen's first big musical production, *Broadway Melody of 1929*, established the magical formula. Although today we laugh at the pudgy chorus girls trying to "make it big" on Broadway, this Metro Goldwyn Mayer production set the tone for a string of spectaculars that glorified the rialto and imprinted the intersection of Broadway and Forty-second Street in the American mind as the most

The first big Hollywood musical, Broadway Melody of 1929, *featured chubby figures, glittery costumes, and melodramatic poses.* Movie Star News

glorious crossroads in the world. *Broadway Melody of 1935*, starring Eleanor Powell, Robert Taylor, and Jack Benny, pitted a Broadway producer against a New York columnist. The 1938 version presented Powell and Taylor joining forces with Sophie Tucker, Judy Garland, Billy Gilbert, and George Murphy to solve the backstage problems which threaten the opening of a new show. In 1940 *Broadway Melody* featured Fred Astaire and Eleanor Powell as a dance team climbing to the top. The list of these movies is endless. The plots vary slightly, but the main ingredients remain the same: the ups and downs on the road to success, ending on the Great White Way in the obligatory musical spectacular.

Following in the same vein were the *Golddigger* series, *Broadway Rhythm*, *Broadway Serenade*, *Tin Pan Alley*, *Ziegfeld's Follies*, *Earl Carroll's*

The Ziegfeld girl—a Broadway phenomenon immortalized on the screen by Lucille Ball.
Movie Star News

Ginger Rogers (black shorts), Ruby Keeler, and Una Merkel lead the chorus-line rehearsal in Forty-second Street. Movie Star News

Vanities, and, perhaps the best known of the genre, *Forty-second Street.* Backstage problems crop up again, but opening night is a huge success for Ruby Keeler, George Brent, Dick Powell, and Ginger Rogers as they tap down Forty-second Street.

Love stories placed couples in the restaurants and on the dance floors of Times Square's biggest nightclubs. Gangster movies took the audiences into Broadway's gambling houses, back alleys, and speakeasies. *Guys and Dolls,* the musical version of a short story by Damon Runyon, introduced the country to a Times Square population of bootleggers, gamblers, hangers-on, showgirls, and soul savers. *Gypsy* and *The Night They Raided Minsky's* glorified the underbelly of Times Square with an inside view of burlesque. Vaudeville found its finest hours running again on the screen with film biographies of Broadway's finest. *The Al Jolson Story* was met with such enthusiasm that a sequel was rapidly made. Barbra Streisand's Fanny Brice

Broadway gamblers join the showgirl and soul-saver for the Hollywood happy ending in Guys and Dolls, *based on the stories of Damon Runyon.* Movie Star News

brought the boards and marquees to life in *Funny Girl*. One of Hollywood's most glorious portraits featured James Cagney as Broadway's own George M. Cohan. His Times Square tribute, "Give My Regards to Broadway," was again on the nation's lips as movie fans filed up the aisles after seeing *Yankee Doodle Dandy*.

The decay in Times Square itself was first ignored by the movie moguls, who preferred to show the early glamor and dazzle of the Square. In the 1960s, however, Hollywood began to take a more realistic view, and such films as *Midnight Cowboy* and, a decade later, *Taxi Driver*, illustrated the decay, violence, and depravity which had, by then, become dominant in certain parts of Times Square.

The portrait presented in these films is an accurate appraisal of the decline which has sadly made

Sheet-music cover for George M. Cohan's "Give My Regards to Broadway." Cohan's music and life were later brought to the screen in Yankee Doodle Dandy, with James Cagney portraying Cohan. Theatre Collection, Museum of the City of New York

much of the Square a monument to human blight. Ironically, the current state of the area harks back to the movie camera that preserved its glories. From the 1930s on, the potboiler movies attracted customers with lurid posters, cutouts, photographs, and loud, rough barkers who hustled the audience with the gory details of their films. When these films played along Forty-second Street, they changed the face of the street with their advertising and the people who were attracted by it.

Even more significant to the changes in Times Square were court decisions regarding the nature of pornography. *I Am Curious Yellow* began an above-

Movie marquees of the
'40s along the Forty-
second Street "strip."
New York Public Library
Picture Collection

Burlesque was the
popular attraction that
paved the way for the
porno movie along
Forty-second Street.
New York Public Library
Picture Collection

Such sideshow attractions as Ripley's Believe-It-or-Not Museum began to filter into the Square in the 1950s. New York Public Library Picture Collection

ground business that had been previously relegated to adult book stores and peep shows. Today the marquees of Forty-second Street, Eighth Avenue, and other sections of Times Square advertise the delights of *Dirty Baby Rosemary, The Farmer's Daughter, Wet Lace, Hot and Spicy Pizza Girls, Boys of Venice, Grease Monkeys,* and other explicit, hard-core pornography.

The old vaudeville pros might well argue that Adolph Zukor's boast would be best changed to "show me any other industry that has done so much *to* Broadway." There is no question, however, that from early nickelodeon houses, to the glorious movie palaces, and to the X-rated theaters, the impact of the motion picture on the fate and fortunes of Times Square has been enormous.

Let There Be Neon

It began with the New Year of 1905. A photograph on the front page of the January 1, 1905 *New York Times* showed newly named Times Square filled with people. Under a headline proclaiming BIG NEW YEAR FETE AT TIMES SQUARE, the paper described the event:

> From base to dome the giant structure was alight—a torch to usher in the newborn, a funeral pyre for the old, which pierced the very heavens.
>
> Broadway had been waiting for the signal. The instant the first flash on the Times Tower showed, a great shout went up, and an ear-splitting blast was sounded from the horns of the myriad merrymakers on the streets below. . . .
>
> Never was a New Year's Eve more joyously celebrated. The streets were crowded almost as darkness set in. Broadway seemed the thoroughfare to which all faces turned, and about every man, woman, and child who put foot upon the street at one time or another during the evening, visited Times Square. As early as nine o'clock the square was packed, and when the time approached when another year should be inscribed upon the century book, the crush was so great that progress was well nigh impossible in any direction.

Thus was born a New York City tradition which continues to this day. The fireworks used for that first celebration have since been banned by City ordinance, but they have been replaced with an illuminated globe that has become the symbol for the New Year across the country. Although thousands crowd the Square to celebrate there, millions more watch the ball descend on television.

The annual celebration—practically an internationally known event—was originally planned to welcome 1905 and the *New York Times* to its new home in the triangle now called Times Square. Thus the *Times* began the tradition of celebration

The financial depression of the 1930s does little to dampen the enthusiasm of this crowd celebrating the New Year in Times Square. **Museum of the City of New York**

in Times Square. In 1910, shortly after setting the precedent for New Year's Eve celebrations, it unconsciously created another Times Square institution which drew the enormous crowds into the triangle. Although owner Adolph Ochs had traditionally downplayed such mass-appeal "news" as sporting events, the managing editor of the newspaper, Carl Van Anda, persuaded Ochs to allow round-by-round bulletins of the Jim Jeffries-Jack Johnson fight in Nevada to be posted on a board affixed to a second-story window. About thirty thousand people gathered to follow the match, and the first stage in the evolution of the *Times* news ribbon began. In 1919 an electric scoreboard was installed to inform the crowds of the outcome of the Cincinnati-Chicago World Series (the one rumored to have been fixed by Broadway gambler Arnold

The curious gather round the theatrical volunteers who provided entertainment during the Liberty Bond drives of World War I. Wide World Photos

Rothstein). A sea of ten thousand straw hats flowed across the Square to follow the ringside bulletins of the Jack Dempsey-Georges Carpentier 1921 bout.

Along with sports results, crowds poured into Times Square to participate in various morale-building events that were initiated during World War I. The *Times,* of course, drew people who wanted to follow the latest reports from the European front. Broadway did its part in shaping yet another New York tradition by presenting live entertainment in the Square just above the Times Tower. Designed to boost war-time spirits, as well as the sale of war bonds, the entertainment was provided by big stars of the day on stages and in band boxes built in the triangle facing the Tower.

In 1928, to report that year's presidential election results, the *Times* inaugurated a sophisticated electric board that announced the news in a ribbon of flashing lights. The 1928 election was a blow to New York's great hero, Governor Al Smith, who was

The 1932 presidential election brought crowds into the Square to follow the returns that took Franklin D. Roosevelt to the White House. The event was to be repeated in 1936, 1940, and 1944.
New York Public Library Picture Collection

defeated by Herbert Hoover. But better news arrived in 1932, when the disgruntled crowds, suffering from the effects of economic depression, gathered to watch Hoover's defeat by Franklin Roosevelt, and three successive elections saw Roosevelt's portrait mounted on the Times building as the returns came pouring in.

The 14,800 amber bulbs in the board were capable of 261,925,664 flashes an hour, and the tradition of the news ribbon was maintained long after the *Times* deserted its Tower. Finally, in 1978, operating expenses became too high, and the bulbs which brought the news to Times Square were extinguished.

The Times ribbon, a tradition, continues to bring the latest news to the Square, although the crowds no longer gather. Collection of the author

The *Times* news ribbon brought with it a new technique in electric display and opened a new age of light in Times Square—the Great White Way was to become the greatest light spectacle in the world. Although the glitter of theater marquees had long lured New Yorkers to the crossroads, it was advertising that gave Times Square the brilliant glow its citizens came to love.

Electric advertising illumination was no stranger to New York City. The first electric sign appeared on Broadway in 1897 to advertise the "ocean breezes" of Coney Island for the rialto patrons in Madison Square. The Floradora Sextette, outlined in carbon bulbs, "danced" across the facade of the Casino Theater at Broadway and Thirty-eighth Street, and actress Maxine Elliott was the first to actually "see her name in lights" along Broadway. But it was not until advertising rolled into Times Square with its extravagant electric billboards that it became the spectacle for which New York City is known.

Early outdoor advertising in the Longacre. Museum of the City of New York

The zoning laws in the area were adapted to permit larger displays than those allowed elsewhere, and, within certain limits of safety, the display boards were allowed to tower as high as the supporting structure would allow. The sky became the limit.

The first large electric display in the area, the great-grandfather of the largest and most popular of all the Times Square spectacles, had been on the west side of the Square, between Forty-fourth and Forty-fifth streets. Here the Wrigley Chewing Gum Company had erected a fanciful fountain in light. Embellished with frills and crowned with a colorful pair of peacocks, the display had soared four stories into the air and was a delightful display for theater patrons from 1917 to the early 1920s. By the thirties, Wrigley's had moved across the street to the Bond Clothing Store, where the sparkling fountain was replaced with a block-long Art Deco display of the sea—complete with bubbling fish and the Wrigley's boy floating atop a pack of spearmint gum (the pack

The Wrigley extravaganza of the 1920s. Collection of the author

of gum was slightly larger than a city bus of the era).

As progress continued its march, the fish made way for the location's owners, Bond Clothing, to hawk their own wares on top of their building. Two giant figures, a male and a female, loomed five stories up from the top of the Bond building. The publicity surrounding the official lighting of the display created a furor over the state of nudity of the Art Deco figures before the light showed the filmy draperies in which they were clad. A small waterfall flowed subtly between them. The figures graced the Square for a decade before what may well be the greatest of all Times Square spectaculars came on the scene.

During the 1950s the figures were removed from the building and replaced by gargantuan bottles of Pepsi-Cola. The bottles, as large as the figures,

would have required 7,812 gallons of Pepsi to actually fill them. The falls between the giant bottles
were expanded, and the entire display was lit with
enough wattage to supply the Brooklyn Dodgers
with the million watts required for two night games.
A supply of 10,000 gallons of water was constantly
recycled to create the effect of 50,000 gallons of
water flowing over the falls every minute. Pre-
cautionary measures required 3,000 gallons of
antifreeze for the winter and a vacuum system
to prevent strong winds from drenching the
pedestrians and traffic below.

The Bond giants and Pepsi-Cola waterfalls were
a result of the combined efforts of conceptual de-
signer Douglas Leigh and artisans Artkraft and
Strauss. The names of Leigh and Artkraft have been
found on the mammoth displays in Times Square

This display required 10,000 gallons of water to keep the falls flowing. Collection of the author

for decades. Leigh, who entered the world of advertising when he accepted a job with the St. Moritz Hotel, has now branched out into architectural lighting and is responsible for the Parisian-style illumination of such landmarks as Grand Central Station, the Empire State Building, and the Chrysler Building.

The firm of Artkraft and Strauss was formed when electrician Jacob Starr joined forces with Benjamin Strauss in a company which produced theatrical cards and posters. The first outdoor displays done by Artkraft in the 1920s were cut from sheetmetal and illuminated with gas from behind. Their workshop, now located in a huge warehouse below the elevated West Side Drive, was originally on the site of the Castro Convertible showroom at the northern end of the Times Square triangle.

Even the snow couldn't dim the glow of Times Square during the winter of 1940. International News Photo

The displays created by Leigh and Artkraft illuminated New York from the early twentieth century to the present. Although the Pepsi-Cola waterfalls was the best known and most spectacular of the Times Square displays, there were countless others to delight and entertain the passersby with the best free show in town. The most exciting and successful displays featured constant repetition of one motion: the Maxwell House coffee cup dripped, but never to the last drop; Johnny Walker covered forty-four miles a night with his twenty-foot stride; and the Anheuser Busch eagle flapped its wings in perpetual flight across Broadway.

Each advertising extravaganza vied with the others for size, intricacy of design, and location—the optimum display spot being the northern end of the Square where the triangle broadens. Budweiser's

Clydesdales pulling a wagon of beer barrels took forty-eight separate drawings in the Artkraft workshop to produce their endless prance. They towered five stories above the Square. TWA built a model of its Super Constellation which was one-third the actual size. With a fuselage of forty-six feet and a wing span of forty-eight feet, it sailed six stories high. Little Lulu hopped about an eight-story display pulling Kleenex from a box. It took thirty-two acetate copies of her, outlined in neon, to produce the effect.

The most outstanding display in Times Square today is the Spectacolor board on the blunted tip of One Times Square, the former Times Tower. Programmed on a computer, it produces the effect of a color cartoon for general advertisers and can be rented by anyone who wishes to have his name or message in lights for thirty seconds on Broadway. Artkraft designed the predecessor of that sign, of which they are particularly proud, in 1939—the Wonder Bread display which was achieved with holes punched over a variety of colored backgrounds.

Not all of the best-remembered displays depended on light. Deodorant cans sprayed mist into the air, music poured onto the streets, twelve-inch soap bubbles floated across the Square, and following close behind the Pepsi waterfalls in popularity, the Camel man blew one perfect smoke ring after another every twenty seconds. (His total cigarette consumption would have amounted to four cartons a day!) The Camel display was a result of the imposed dimming of lights during World War II. It was discovered that the glow emanating from Times Square alone produced a light strong enough miles out at sea to outline American ships against the skyline. When several were torpedoed by German submarines, the government ordered the lights above street level turned out in Times Square.

There was certainly no subtlety to these landmarks. They twinkled, danced, whirled, swirled, and leaped across the streets and avenues to the constant astonishment of drivers and pedestrians. However, not everyone enjoyed the free show taking place in the Square, and the advertising displays have been criticized as cheap, vulgar, ugly,

The Camel man smoked four cartons of cigarettes a day to produce the fluffy rings that floated into the Square. **New York Public Library Picture Collection**

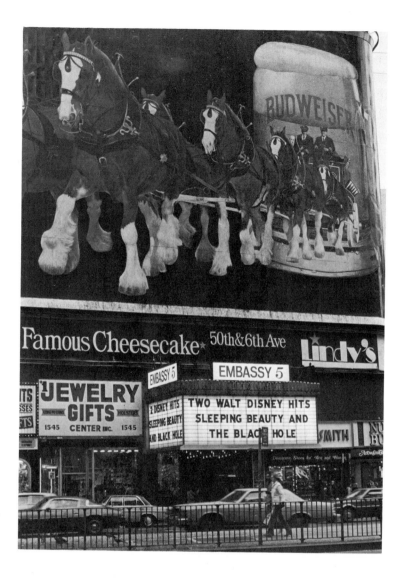

This giant-sized painted ad is becoming typical of an energy-conscious Times Square. Daniel Meltzer

insulting, wasteful of light, and lacking in artistic sense. While much of that criticism is valid, it is hard to think of Times Square without that incredible show of lights.

Times Square without lights? Unthinkable, yet during the late 1960s and early 1970s the fantastic displays began to disappear. In 1975, when New York began to feel the effects of the energy crunch, most of the outdoor displays consisted of huge painted billboards—no less creative in their execution, but certainly less dazzling and intense than their predecessors.

John Starr, of Artkraft, sees the future of advertising in Times Square making use of illumination sources other than electricity. He credits the decline of the extravaganzas to the growth of advertising in other media, recalling that, during its peak, the Square was a media center like no other in the world. At that time news could not be found on television, but the *Times* news ribbon, the theaters, restaurants, stores, and, perhaps more than anything else, the lights, drew people like a giant magnet into the heart of Times Square.

Passing Through:
World War II

The 1940s saw yet another boom period in Times Square as the war years generated larger income for the Depression-racked citizenry. Although the United States was not officially threatened or involved, the "prewar jitters" hung heavily in the air, and a spirit of carefree abandon pervaded. A "you can't take it with you" attitude brought customers into the theaters, restaurants, and nightclubs to eat, drink, and be merry as they had not since the Roaring Twenties. The pace was fast and, once again, the times were hot.

The nightclub circuit underwent drastic change, catering to the crowds' insistence on lavish entertainment. While the clubs of the late thirties provided a luxurious backdrop for patrons to create their own fun, in the 1940s a forced gaiety produced the necessary forgetfulness of common fears. The clubs provided big-name entertainment and pulled in enormous profits. Jimmy Durante and Joe E. Lewis kept the crowds laughing while the bands of Kay Kyser and Tommy Dorsey provided the music. Duke Ellington packed them into the Hurricane on Broadway, and George Price ruled as king of the Latin Quarter. (By 1945 the Latin Quarter was one of the top money-makers in the nightclub business, grossing $45,000 a week, followed closely by Billy Rose's Diamond Horseshoe at $40,000.)

The prewar period was the first upturn for vaudeville since its drastic decline during the Depression. Interest in the stage show was revived, and headliners such as Sophie Tucker, Durante, the Andrews Sisters, and the Inkspots hit the boards during the war. However, top billing still went to the

BILLY ROSE'S
DIAMOND HORSESHOE

PROGRAMME 25¢

A program from the Diamond Horseshoe, which flourished in the prewar boom of the late 1930s. Collection of the author

big bands, like those of the Dorseys or Glenn Miller, and the singers with them. Thus was born the career of one Frank Sinatra, who spiraled to superstardom after his engagement with Tommy Dorsey. In 1944 his performance at the Paramount brought thousands of screaming bobby-soxers to swoon in Times Square. The Roxy, Paramount, Capitol, and Strand—homes for the huge new stage shows—competed constantly for the headliners, paying higher salaries than ever before. The Roxy paid $37,000 for a show featuring Danny Kaye and the Tommy Tucker Band. The Paramount countered and topped the Roxy by paying $40,000 to such names as Jack Benny, Bob Hope, Milton Berle, and the team of Dean Martin and Jerry Lewis.

Times Square was, once again, glittering with the light of the stars of the day. Servicemen in transit poured into its streets in search of a good time in the Big Apple. New York was the transportation hub for the men traveling between base, home, and front. Though the stay was brief, nearly every soldier, flier, sailor, and marine passed through the City on his way to places unknown. For some, it was the last great fling before departure to foreign shores; others made steady pilgrimages to the City when on leave from American bases, and some came home to visit the New York they'd left behind. For many of these men it was their first trip to the razzle-dazzle town, and for too many it was their last. But whatever their reason or destination, they all came to Times Square.

One Brooklyn-born soldier on leave explained to the *New York Post:*

In 1944, the hottest musical sensation in town played the Paramount, as 25,000 teenage fans filled the theater and the Square to scream for Frank Sinatra. Wide World Photos

The streets around Times Square provided a last fling for servicemen on their way to foreign ports. **Museum of the City of New York**

The first thing, of course, is to say hello to my mother. Next, I'll have breakfast—a big one. And then, I'll go to Times Square and stand there practically all day smelling the frankfurters and breathing in the cold air from all those air-conditioned movie houses. And one of the things I want to do is yoohoo at every pretty girl who passes by.

And pass by they did. Those years between 1941 and 1945 saw unprecedented crowds in the Square. Men in uniform lined the streets, filled the theaters and restaurants, visited the nightclubs, and contributed to the party atmosphere for four years. The attractions were many and they appealed to every taste. New York City's beautiful women passed through the Square on their way to work, shopping and sometimes winking back at the young servicemen. Forty-second Street was ablaze with every popular movie of the day. A free show always drew crowds as the Broadway headliners again did their bit for the war bond drives. Throughout the Square the hucksters abounded, calling patrons into the stores sandwiched between the theaters. The street hustlers offered an amazing array of forbidden delights. War-time fuel and food shortages, blackouts,

Free show to sell war bonds in 1944. The goal: a bond for every theater seat in Times Square. Associated Press

and the liquor shortage didn't seem to dampen the spirits of the Times Square revelers. When the midnight curfew, imposed by the War Mobilization Board, caused nightclub owners to groan, patriot Toots Shor summed up the spirit of the day, "Any crum bum what can't get drunk by midnight just ain't tryin'." Mayor Fiorello LaGuardia saved the day when he announced that, after all, "New York is still New York" and extended the curfew to 1:00 A.M.

Broadway's stage offerings included *My Sister Eileen, Arsenic and Old Lace, Winged Victory, The Corn Is Green, I Remember Mama, The Skin of Our Teeth, Carousel, Harvey, The Glass Menagerie,* and the biggest hit of the decade, *Oklahoma.*

But for the servicemen interested in seeing the glittering stars of Broadway in closer quarters than ever before or since, the Stage Door Canteen offered the greatest entertainment to be found in New York. The biggest names on movie marquees, the-

Lights above street level were prohibited during the blackouts of World War II. **Museum of the City of New York**

ater playbills, phonograph records, and bandstands came to entertain, dance, serve coffee, chat, and build the morale of the men passing so quickly through its doors. From Milton Berle to the Duchess of Windsor, the ranks of the entertainment and social elite poured into the canteen in a space donated by the Shuberts below Sardi's Restaurant on West Forty-fourth Street. It was Broadway's contribution to the servicemen and, in true Broadway style, it was dazzling. The canteen was immortalized in the Sol Lesser film *Stage Door Canteen.* The film featured all available Broadway stars of the day and the songs of the popular crooner Lannie Ross (who, it might be added, was selected by Lesser over the young newcomer offered by his agent as the greatest upcoming star of the day— Lesser was not convinced and Frank Sinatra lost the part).

The Stage Door Canteen was only a small portion of the contribution made by Broadway during the

*The Stage Door Canteen
—where servicemen
danced with the stars.*
Museum of the City of
New York

war years. The efforts harked back to World War I when the theaters and performers pledged their full support of American servicemen and U.S. military involvement on the European front. During World War I the theaters had opened their doors to the "four-minute-men" who appeared between the acts to sell bonds. The Palace alone had collected $750,000 for the Liberty loan program.

Irving Berlin was awarded a well-deserved Legion of Merit after producing the immensely successful musicals *Yip Yip Yaphank* during World War I and *This Is the Army* during World War II. Both shows had all-soldier casts, and proceeds were turned over to the United States government. *This Is the Army* (including the proceeds from the film version) grossed $10 million for Uncle Sam.

World War I had also spawned the predecessors

of the modern USO [United Services Organization] camp shows, when Liberty theaters opened on U.S. bases. George M. Cohan called on his fellow performers to travel to the European front with his newly formed Over There League. In 1940 President Roosevelt requested that one organization serve the armed forces. The resulting USO was a combined effort of the National Jewish Welfare Board, the Catholic Community Services, the YMCA, YWCA, the Salvation Army, and Travelers Aid to create a comforting place for the serviceman away from home. Here he could relax, socialize, and meet both other servicemen and local volunteers from the USO base town. Of the twelve centers located in the New York metropolitan area, the most popular was the Times Square center.

World War II brought outdoor entertainment for bond drives; a Crack-a-Jap cocktail offered in one Times Square theater, consisting of a ten-cent defense stamp and a glass of water; the theater campaign for junk and salvage; free theater tickets for servicemen; and a benefit at Madison Square Garden organized by Billy Rose that raised $10 million for the USO. In every respect Broadway did its part.

Perhaps the most significant contribution of Times Square in those years was a result, quite accidentally, of its existence. Times Square had always drawn crowds, and the war years were no exception. Servicemen came to visit, New Yorkers came to watch the uniformed heroes, and all came to follow the reports from the front on the news ribbon circling the Times Tower.

In the late afternoon of August 15, 1945, an agonizing vigil began beneath the news ribbon on the Times Tower as 200,000 people awaited confirmation of the rumor which had kept hopes and fears mounting for five interminable days. As the afternoon dragged on, their ranks began to swell until, by seven o'clock, 750,000 strong, they blocked all traffic between Fortieth and Forty-eighth streets along Broadway and waited quietly, fearfully.

At 7:03 it came. The lights of the *Times* ribbon repeated over and over the most joyous message ever brought to Broadway:

OFFICIAL—TRUMAN ANNOUNCES JAPANESE SURRENDER

As the message flickered around the ribbon, total silence fell just briefly while the enormity of the message sunk in, and then a shout went up from Times Square that was heard on the Hudson River, First Avenue, up to Columbus Circle (Fifty-ninth Street), and down to Herald Square (Thirty-fourth Street). It was a spontaneous, wild, miraculous release and, although all across America celebrations broke out, there were none to equal the joyous display in Times Square.

For hours after the announcement was made the revelry continued as the crowd grew. By 10:00 P.M. 2 million people were packed solidly from Fortieth to Forty-eighth streets between Sixth and Eighth

Opposite: On August 15, 1945, an anxious crowd gathers to await the news that will spark the Square's greatest celebration. **Wide World Photos**

Glad celebration of the war's end. **New York Public Library Picture Collection**

avenues. They tossed hats, boxes, packages, and flags into the air as a steady stream of confetti, paper, and streamers fell from windows above. They shouted, whistled, screamed, danced, cried, waved flags, and blew horns. The City provided a cacaphony of fire-engine clangs and police-siren wails as the noise grew ever louder and more joyous. The *Times* described it in the next morning edition: "The victory roar beat upon the eardrums until it numbed the senses."

The Big Apple became just another small town as the revelers in the Square kissed and embraced everyone in sight. Trucks filled with merrymakers, horns blowing, pulled through Broadway and Seventh Avenue and cars, filled with passengers, took on more as passersby jumped on running boards, hoods, and roofs in a spontaneous parade. As the news flashed across the screen of Radio City Music Hall the audience of six thousand rose as one, cheering and deserting the theater for the exuberant revelry in Times Square. The crowds poured into the Square on buses, subways, cars, and on foot.

It seemed that, even more than before, all roads led to Times Square, and the stroke of midnight found 1,500,000 people celebrating the greatest moment the Square had ever known.

Opposite: The celebration continues well into the night. Museum of the City of New York

7

Honky-Tonk Town

Times Square reached its moment of crowning glory on V-J Day, with the celebration that marked the end of World War II. Soon, the boom of the early 1940s came to an abrupt halt. Gone from the American scene were the huge profits of the war years. Defense workers who had spent their inflated salaries on the escapist entertainment in Times Square went back to their prewar professions and incomes. Riveting housewives returned to their homes. The cold war set in, and an economic recession set the cautious financial tone.

Times Square in the subdued 1950s still sparkled with the lively appeal that made the area "Carnival Crossroads." Wide World Photos

The 1950s saw the beginnings of the most drastic changes in Times Square since Hammerstein first set foot in the Longacre. With the heady thrill of V-J Day now a distant memory, Sen. Joseph McCarthy stormed across the headlines. His search for Communists and fellow travelers took his investigations into theater, film, and literary circles, casting a long shadow over the entertainment industry. The real and imagined threat of communism, coupled with the economic downturn, led to a serious and careful turn of mind. People were not interested in the lavish entertainment that had been so readily available in Times Square in the past. Slowly the landmarks of the 1930s and 1940s faded from the Square.

All forms of entertainment were hit hard by sagging attendance and profits. The doors to the most popular nightclubs closed throughout the late forties and early fifties. The Big Bands that packed the night spots and stages of Broadway were no longer popular; they were replaced, first, by jazz combos, which thrived in more intimate surroundings, and then by rock 'n' roll groups. Box-office receipts were down at legitimate theaters, where high prices always suffered in periods of recession. The movies also suffered from the communist scare and subsequent investigations. The frenzied tomorrow-we-may-die attitude of the war years yielded, in reaction, to a psychological and financial need to stay quietly at home. In the 1950s middle-class New Yorkers began leaving the City for suburban life. As vaudeville had been threatened by the movies, movies now were put on the defensive by the American passion for a new entertainment form— television. Families could be entertained in the security and comfort of their own homes at little expense. No trip from the suburbs to the City was required. Comedy, drama, music, and the latest news arrived instantaneously on the home screen, and the theater, movies, and entertainment in Times Square suffered.

The decline of Forty-second Street that had

By the late 1940s, the movie palaces of Times Square were making way for the growing phenomenon of television. New York Public Library Picture Collection

begun in the 1930s increased in pace and severity. The grinders exchanged gangster movies and war sagas for the psychological thrillers and horror movies which gained popularity in the fifties. *The Creature from the Black Lagoon* and *Godzilla* peered onto the former glory of Forty-second Street from their marquee perches. The grinders spread from Forty-second Street onto Broadway and Seventh Avenue, and although many theaters on these avenues continued their policy of showing first-rate films, the general atmosphere was predominated by the cheap houses.

The amusement park attractions—Skee-Ball, Fascination, pinball—continued to prosper but did little to improve the image of Times Square and New York City as a whole. Child's Paramount Restaurant, which opened in 1927 just in time for the Big Band era, was replaced by Ripley's Believe-It-or-Not Museum, first cousin to the freak-show attractions of Hubert's Flea Circus. By 1953 the Broadway Association complained, "The midway developing in Times Square as a result of the continued intrusion of amusement arcades and garish auction shops is earning New York the reputation of

Today's pinball emporium, heir to the honky-tonk tradition of the Square. Daniel Meltzer

Honky-Tonk Town." The association was one of the first to realize that the changes taking place in Times Square reflected the City's image in the eyes of the world.

The growing popularity of television affected Times Square in more ways than decreased movie attendance. The amber bulbs of the news ribbon on the Times Tower continued to flash the latest events into the Square, but the crowds that once gathered to follow the headlines no longer came; they preferred to stay home and watch television news reports. Only on New Year's Eve did tradition continue to draw crowds into the Square.

With the court decisions of the late 1960s and early 1970s came a more tolerant attitude toward pornography, and Times Square, with its rich history of burlesque and prostitution, was ripe for this newly unfettered entertainment form. There is a tendency to view prostitution as a recent phenomenon in the Square, but the fact is that during both world wars prostitution flourished in Times Square, so much so that the World War II Victory Girls were the subject of army training films warning against venereal disease. Recent years have given rise to

The Elegant APRIL SUMERS

Although the format of burlesque has changed since the early years of Times Square, shapely girls in rhinestones still bump and grind on the stages. **Daniel Meltzer**

more blatant and garish solicitation, but the area has always had its share of illicit nightlife, of which today's teenage runaways are a small but pathetic part.

In a paradoxical city, Times Square is still a study of incredible contrasts. During daylight hours the streets of the Square are populated by a cross section of city workers. Beginning in the early morning, the Port Authority Bus Terminal, on Eighth Avenue at Forty-first Street, pours thousands of suburban commuters from every conceivable profession onto the streets of the Square and into the network of subways below. The subways also bring thousands more workers from every borough of New York City into the streets, as office workers, garment-center employees, local merchants, waiters, waitresses, restaurateurs, and newspaper and television people head for the buildings of the surrounding area. By lunch hour these workers are joined by entertainers, theater employees, local residents, tourists, matinee patrons, street peddlers, hustlers, and mounted police going about their appointed rounds. By midnight, when the workers have long since returned to their homes in the outer boroughs and suburbs, the final curtain has fallen, and the dishwashers are clearing the dinner remains, the Square is taken over by its less savory types—drug pushers, male and female prostitutes, runaways, derelicts, junkies, pimps.

Perpetual motion on the sidewalks of New York's busiest spot. **Daniel Meltzer**

Simple Simon awaits a taste from the neon pieman, as the night crowds begin to assemble north of the Square.
Daniel Meltzer

The splendid facades of the district's theaters, many newly refurbished, stand just around the corner from the blaring music advertising live sex shows. Theater patrons hail cabs and hurry to parked cars through a sea of hustlers, drug peddlers, and prostitutes. Just a few doors away from Rod Swenson's Show World, where simulated sex is the draw, stands one of New York's largest religious bookstores. Young people carrying transistors blasting disco snake their way through the crowded streets. Shakespeare often plays just a block away from *Black Leather Boys.* The mix of human elements is incongruous, but it does reflect the range of attractions that draw people to Times Square, and it does speak for the glamor and garishness that Times Square symbolizes in the public mind.

Through all the changes in Times Square, the Broadway stage still reigns as the symbol and showplace of the American theater. Recent seasons have delivered such outstanding musical and dramatic fare as *Annie, Children of a Lesser God, A Chorus*

Line, Dancin', The Elephant Man, Evita, Morning's at Seven, and *They're Playing Our Song.* Harking back to the earlier days of the rialto are shows like *Ain't Misbehavin'* (a musical salute to jazz great Fats Waller), *Barnum* (a biographical extravaganza of P. T. Barnum), *Forty-second Street* (the song-and-dance spectacular of Broadway), a marvelous revival of *Peter Pan,* and *Sugar Babies* (a portrait of burlesque from 1900–1930).

Many of the legitimate theaters have been restored and display the ornate glory of their earliest years. The Plymouth, Ethel Barrymore, Morosco,

The magnificent facade of the Lyceum has graced the Square since 1903. Daniel Meltzer

Royale, Music Box, Booth, Lyceum, Imperial, Lunt-Fontanne, Winter Garden, Cort, Longacre, St. James, Shubert, and Broadhurst are but a few of the fine old theaters which still grace Broadway and the West Forties.

Although these theaters are reminders of Broadway's golden age and today are drawing large audiences, the mention of Times Square conjures up an entirely different picture in the public mind. When, in the 1960s, the Forty-second Street strip began to be billed in the media as the worst block in the City, the image of Times Square became one of violent crime, illicit sex, vagrancy, drug traffic, and pornography. Unfortunately, this picture is not entirely inaccurate. Business crowds may bustle through the Square in the daylight hours, but certain sections of the area are menacing to even the most hardened New Yorkers.

A stroll down Forty-second Street between Seventh and Eighth avenues provides a graphic portrait of Times Square's sleazier nature. Just as the theaters on Forty-fourth Street are fine examples of architectural beauty and former glory, "the strip" is a cross section of the elements which make up the new image of the Square.

Most readily apparent are the large groups of young black and Latin men who, at first glance, would appear to be hanging out in front of the theaters and storefronts along the strip. There have been such groups in Times Square since the 1920s, but earlier there was little that was frightening or threatening about the young men. They conversed and ogled the women passing by but in no way interfered with the pedestrian flow or altered the atmosphere of the area. With the advent of the Depression, however, the hangers-on were more likely to be the unemployed who, in desperation accosted passersby for handouts. Pickpocketing became common. The young men along the strip today are there for any one of several reasons: drug traffic, sale of stolen goods, male prostitution, or the con games which proliferate in the Square. Studies

Sampling some of New York's plentiful cuisine.
Daniel Meltzer

have shown that, even during daylight hours, women feel particularly insecure traversing that strip. The male population outnumbers women three to one in the daytime and seven to one at night. A close look at the variety of hustles offered by these young men makes it clear why women avoid Forty-second Street.

The only relatively passive members of the Times Square hustle are the vagrants and derelict alcoholics who sometimes panhandle on the strip and in the surrounding area but are more frequently found sleeping in the doorways of office buildings and theater entrances on the side streets. They are sometimes a part of the bottle gangs that gather around the Eighth Avenue bars and behind the Forty-second Street theaters on Forty-first and Forty-third to pass a shared bottle. Bottles of Night Train, the beverage of choice with the gangs, litter the sidewalks and gutters.

Peddlers along the strip sell everything from women's dresses to small electronic equipment. All merchandise is geared to the most popular fashions and fads, making for a quick turnover of goods. These peddlers are always on the move, changing location frequently with a constant eye out for the

police. Unlicensed to sell along the streets, they usually are pushing goods stolen from local stores and the nearby garment district.

Also on the move are the sidewalk con men, who attract a surprisingly large number of marks when you consider the age-old premise of games like Three-Card Monte—a variation of the shell game practiced on the unwary for years. The object of the game is to pick the red queen from three artfully shuffled cards—a feat so rarely accomplished that the Monte men gross $100 to $200 on an average day. Cilo is another game popular with the street cons. It depends on dice loaded to favor the operator.

Drug dealers make up the largest group of independent businessmen along the strip. Loose joints and bags of marijuana are the most popular offer-

"Watch me, now. Watch me—," says the three-card monte dealer. Daniel Meltzer

ings, with dealers averaging a profit of $100 a day or more. However, customers can easily satisfy a variety of desires, with Tuinol, heroin, Quaaludes, Valium, amphetamines, hallucinogens, and cocaine readily available. To decrease the possibility of arrest and prosecution, the dealers rarely carry more than small amounts of their product and never give samples or allow a look at their wares. Prices (and quality) are usually below the market in other sections of the city and rip-offs are frequent.

Times Square's gay community is represented along the strip by homosexual misfits, the ex-convicts who do not easily fit into the educated, middle-class groups in Greenwich Village and the Upper East Side. Male prostitutes, usually young men ranging in age from sixteen to twenty, work the strip side by side with the dealers and peddlers, loitering in doorways and making eye contact with

Handsome young men in celluloid or in the flesh are readily available in the Square. Daniel Meltzer

possible clients. Often they can be seen carrying on discreet conversations, after which they eventually wander off to a room or hotel for a "drink."

Times Square is crowded with all these street-smart hustlers, each selling his individual brand of thrills. For the street people, the strip is home—a place to work, to socialize, to eat, drink, and sleep. The thrill of the unexpected, as well as the promise of profit, attracts and keeps them in the Square.

The anonymity provided by the crowds who traverse the Square, the easy access to public transportation, and the atmosphere created by the grinders and sex parlors make Forty-second Street a prime location for these young entrepreneurs. As one Times Square worker put it,

If you city planners set out to make a place for dope peddlers, you couldn't plan anything as good as Times Square. I get off the bus from Detroit without a penny in my pocket. I walk up to the blood bank on Forty-second Street, where I sell a pint of my blood, take the money, and go just four doors away where I can buy me a knife. I use the money left over to go into one of them all-night movies, where I slit open the back pocket of the first sleeping drunk I see. I take his money down to the street, buy myself an ounce of smoke, find myself a doorway, and begin selling. I've been in town less than an hour and I'm already in business.

It would appear that as long as there is a market for the drugs, stolen merchandise, and other goods peddled in the Square, the traffic will grow.

The grinders began by attracting a lower-class male audience that frequented other Times Square amusements and used the bars and streets to hang out. When the movie houses began to stay open twenty-four hours they made Forty-second Street the perfect location for vagrants, derelicts, and loiterers. The street became home to a group which depended on the hustle for its livelihood.

Many claim that the growth of sex-related businesses in the Square is responsible for drug traffic and the petty crime that is its logical accompaniment. Certainly those persons first drawn to burlesques, then to the more clandestine "peeps," and today to the X-rated films, live sex shows, and mas-

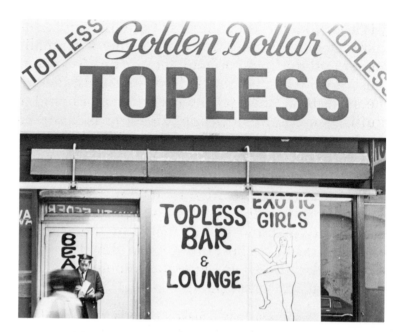

Timeless allure of the area: an endless succession of girls.
Daniel Meltzer

sage parlors represented excellent potential marks for the street trade. Tourists and commuters who constantly pass through are another good source of customers.

The skin trade has always been active in the Square in a variety of forms, the oldest of which is, of course, prostitution. Even before the rialto had stretched to Forty-second Street, the moral guardians of the city complained of the "iniquitous concert saloons" dotting Broadway. In the mid-1800s streetwalkers paraded Broadway from Canal Street to Madison Square Garden, and Bishop Simpson of the Methodist Episcopal Church indignantly charged in a sermon that there were "more prostitutes than Methodists" in New York. Police Superintendent John Kennedy contested the charges and reassured New Yorkers with these statistics: There were, at the time, only 621 houses of prostitution, 99 houses of assignation, 75 concert saloons, and 3,300 public prostitutes (including 747 waiter-girls in concert saloons).

Today the prostitutes have moved west from Broadway to Eighth Avenue, where buses arriving in the Port Authority Terminal deliver a steady stream of customers. Most of the women working this area from the bars between Fortieth and Forty-first streets, go hand in glove with that other phenomenon—the Times Square pimp. The bus station thus serves another purpose for the skin trade, as the small-time pimps (known in the life as simps) cruise the building seeking teenage runaways from the Midwest who have earned Eighth Avenue the title "Minnesota Strip."

The women, gaudier and more ragged than the prostitutes in other quarters of the City, operate blatantly along the avenue, taking their johns—customers—to cars, trucks, doorways, and hotel rooms. They even turn "tunnel tricks," providing their services while driving through the Lincoln Tunnel, which links New York to New Jersey.

Closely related to female prostitution is the industry comprised of adult films and bookstores, peep shows, emporiums selling sex toys and devices, and live sex shows. Many women who do not actively solicit customers perform strip dances or live sex acts with partners in such "theaters" as Show World or the Pussycat. Many peeps feature a variety of live sexual acts. Women pose on revolving platforms, perform special requests, and listen to the fantasies of patrons who watch from glass-windowed booths.

Adult films, peeps, and bookstores have thrived in Times Square since the relaxation of regulations governing the sale of so-called pornographic material. Forty-second Street, between Sixth and Eighth avenues, houses seven sex-oriented theaters with twice that number scattered throughout the Square, although, as live shows have gained in popularity, there has been a significant decline in their attendance. It would appear, however, that the trend in sex-oriented entertainment will culminate in the emporium which offers books, magazines, sexual devices, and peep booths featuring a large selection of films and live performances all under the same roof. Show World, on Eighth Avenue, is typical of these new shopping malls for sex entertainment.

Some years ago, when she made her last appear-

The "peeps," where 25¢ will give the customer a glimpse of "the naked and the live." Daniel Meltzer

ance on the Broadway stage, the once-infamous Mae West visited a Times Square peep show. Her verdict: "It'll never go—no sex appeal." Time has, unfortunately, proved her wrong. The trade in flesh and sex is a million-dollar industry in New York. The tiny storefronts on Times Square which display their books and magazines pay rentals of up to $50,000 a year and still manage handsome profits. The tax dollars paid to the City are high, but both the City and community would be happy to be rid of these movies and shops which offend the middle class.

The owners of the flesh parlors, bolstered by court decisions, ask to whom the business is offensive. Certainly, they say, not to the customers who provide the enormous profits. They quickly point out that those offended by the marquees, displays, and handbills need only avoid the area or avert their eyes. They remind critics that they have not created the market for their goods but merely cater to the existing demand. Complaints about the general

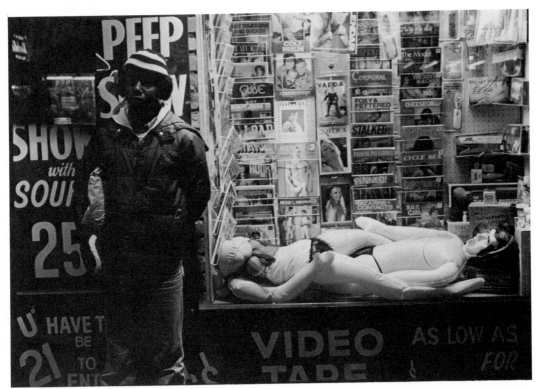

This emporium combines the standard peep with a selection of books to appeal to every sexual taste. **Daniel Meltzer**

seediness of the Square are blamed on the street traffic that the owners claim is unrelated to their businesses.

Several community groups actively fight the sex industry on various levels. Generally these groups emphasize rejuvenation of property, elimination of the sex-oriented businesses in the immediate area, and a crackdown on prostitution and drug sales. Women Against Pornography is a feminist group whose headquarters on Ninth Avenue arranges tours of the local pornographic movie houses, sex shops and live shows to publicize the inherent exploitation and degradation of women by the adult entertainment industry. The community cleanup proposed by other local and civic groups is on a larger scale.

One City agency which has had some success in fighting the influx of pornography to the Square is the Mayor's Midtown Enforcement Project, headed by Carl Weisbrod. The agency was designed to enforce the City ordinances regarding obscenity,

Live nude shows present an alternative to the film peeps for the Times Square customer, but offer no choice to the passerby within hearing range of the amplified broadcasts of the action onstage. **Daniel Meltzer**

building codes, and sanitation. Its surveillance and constant inspection of the sex shops and theaters in the Square has led to the temporary and even permanent closing of several establishments. This is, however, only a stopgap action.

Particularly susceptible to the lure of both prostitution and the sex trade are the thousands of teenage runaways who arrive in New York each year. With no way to support themselves, many of the young people find their way to Times Square, where their lack of experience, education, and emotional stability is an asset. Covenant House, a nonsectarian child care agency headed by Father Bruce Ritter, has nine residences for runaways in crucial areas of Manhattan. The busiest of these centers is Under 21, a twenty-four hour crisis center which takes care of the immediate needs of exploited and runaway children. Ritter estimates that twenty thousand runaways under the age of sixteen are on the streets of New York each year and 60 percent of those who come to him (both male and female) have had some contact with prostitution and pornography.

The young people appearing at Father Ritter's door who have not been involved in the sex industry have supported themselves on the streets with drug sales and petty crime. Although the prostitution, gambling, and drug trade in the area are considered "victimless crimes," with all parties participating voluntarily, there is still an association between these crimes and the violent crimes of junkies, pushers, sexual aberrants, and street hangers-on with no means of financial support.

Police statistics show that the most common serious crime committed in the Times Square area is assault, almost always associated with drug deals gone bad, prostitution (abuse by a pimp or john), vying street hustles, or muggings. Petty theft—mugging, pickpocketing, and purse and jewelry snatching—exists in the Square but is not as prevalent as the public might suspect. The high volume of street and pedestrian traffic along Broadway, Seventh Avenue and Forty-second Street affords a certain degree of immunity from the typical empty-street New York mugging. After the theaters close, however, the darkened side streets of the West Forties are open to street crime, and even during the busy daylight hours, certain areas of the Port Authority Bus Terminal and Eighth Avenue subway station are frighteningly susceptible to theft and assault.

Public protests from local groups and well-publicized pronouncements, such as Transit Authority police labeling of the Eighth Avenue subway station as the "most dangerous in the city," have done little to alleviate the petty thefts, assaults, or victimless crimes. Police openly complain about a judicial system which requires, for prosecution, almost two full days of court and paperwork away from street patrol. Often, offenders who are released on bail or probation reappear on the street in hours.

To step up law enforcement and public protection in the Times Square area, the New York police have initiated Operation Crossroads, which is run out of a police substation on Forty-second Street, across the street from One Times Square. This substation fields eighty uniformed men to patrol the area. Initially the operation had a significant effect on the hustles and petty crimes along the strip but,

A Times Square prostitute solicits along Eighth Avenue. Wide World Pictures

just as the police gained useful information from watching the patterns of the street people, so, too, did the hustlers. They adapted readily to the new schedules of Operation Crossroads and moved to safer locations. The presence of visible numbers of uniformed police in the streets of the Square continues to create the illusion of safety, but even more policemen cannot overcome the problems in the system which have consistently thwarted crime prevention in the area.

Times Square stands today as a monument to the elegance of a glorious past, the capital of a tawdry present, and the vision of an uncertain future. The extraordinary variety of its present population is not new to the Times Square that has seen come and go vaudeville, Broadway, and Hollywood headliners, the crime kingpins of Prohibition, flappers and jitterbuggers, professional beauties and impresarios, stage-door Johnnies and Wall Street tycoons, foreign stars and burlesque queens, servicemen from two wars, and crowds which came to see and be seen in a place like no other in the world. The restoration and preservation of this unique site in New York history should be the goal of the future.

The Future Hope

At present, the future of Times Square is clouded by confusion and uncertainty. No fewer than six different interest groups—community, City, theatrical, retail, real estate, and nonprofit—appear to be working against one another for the common cause of revitalizing Times Square. Without one authoritative spokesman to coordinate both the well-meaning and the self-serving efforts for revitalization, it appears that Forty-second Street will continue to be a battleground, slowly deteriorating for lack of any action.

One of the earliest plans for revitalization of the area prohibits traffic between Fiftieth and Forty-second Streets on both Broadway and Seventh Avenue, thus creating a triangular pedestrian mall. This proposal, under consideration for nearly six years, is, at present, crawling slowly to reality in abbreviated form. The new proposal calls for a bricked pedestrian mall on Broadway between Forty-fifth and Forty-seventh streets. The center of this triangle, the former Times Tower, is the focus for nothing less than four redevelopment possibilities from different sources. The most obvious option leaves the building as it is, continuing its use as awkwardly shaped but well-located office space. Its current owner, Alex Parker, sporting a Mickey Mouse necktie, talks of plans to turn the building into a family entertainment center—a vertical Disneyland. Other projects under consideration involve leveling the building and constructing on its site a tourist information center (now located directly across Forty-second Street on the site of a former peep show). The planners for the City at

Forty-second Street, a nonprofit organization devoted to the revitalization of the area, show models of a beautiful glass subway entrance, visible and well lit, to be built on the site.

One of the many problems facing any plan for cleanup and revitalization is the value of the real estate along Forty-second Street between Seventh and Eighth avenues. Although this block has deteriorated in terms of its use and human population, the properties remain valuable midtown real estate and, in light of proposed redevelopment, the possibility that its value will rise is certainly great. Most of the property owners along the strip recognize the need for restoration, preservation, and revitalization and claim to be willing to make the necessary investments to upgrade their present holdings, but fear the ax of urban renewal.

The Brandt Organization, which owns ten theaters in the Times Square area, has already begun its own restoration project. The Brandts became a business force in Times Square in the late 1920s, when the economic pressures of the Depression

*Opposite: **Drawn in 1911, this is an artist's view of New York's future.** Collection of the author*

The future arrives as the Spectacolor sign on the northern facade of One Times Square beams a message to passing New Yorkers. Daniel Meltzer

boarded the doors of Times Square's legitimate theaters. Recognizing the coming boom in motion pictures, the Brandts acquired many properties in the area and converted them to movie houses. These theaters along with others on the strip, appealed to audiences of mass taste and moderate income. Adventures, horror movies, westerns, thrillers, and sexually suggestive films have been the standard fare of these houses. Many theater owners will flatly denounce these grinders as the single greatest influence in the decline of Times Square.

In 1979, however, the Brandts took a giant step in another direction. The New Apollo, a movie house in the middle of the Forty-second Street strip, was renovated and reopened as the legitimate house it once was, with a new entrance on the "model block" of Forty-third Street. The plans have a built-in adaptation for an entrance on Forty-second Street when the strip is clean enough to once again attract middle-class audiences to legitimate theater on Forty-second Street. The Brandts also restored the magnificently ornate facade of the Lyric Theater on

The mass-appeal movies of the strip. Daniel Meltzer

Forty-third Street, although it still features mass appeal movies on Forty-second Street, where the real entrance of the theater is located.

Vice President of the chain, Robert Brandt, is, however, frightened by the plans proposed by various civic groups. Calling the plan of the City at Forty-second Street group a "thinly disguised land grab for developers and large real-estate interests," he fears for the investments he has made and explains the reluctance of other property owners along the strip to follow the Brandt lead. The risks involved center on property values. The owners of these properties represent one faction in the battle over Forty-second Street. Opposition comes in the form of several groups who favor urban renewal.

Although filled with complexities, the basic concept of urban renewal is simple. The area in question is denounced as "blighted," the properties are then condemned, and the Urban Development Corporation (UDC) steps in to offer compensation to the owners of the condemned properties. The term *offer* is the catch, for the owner has no choice but to accept the compensation set by the UDC. At this point, any outside interest with plans for upgrading the property is eligible to purchase the properties, at a relatively low price, from the UDC.

Since the ultimate goal is the resurrection of Times Square from its present state of decay, the intervention of the UDC is not necessarily negative. But the present property owners claim that the condemnation procedure as it is now outlined is for the entire area, not just random buildings. The price offered to present owners by the UDC is dictated by guidelines based on an average value of sample property valuations in the area.

Such a procedure presents definite risks to the present owners along the strip, who claim that even those buildings which have been restored and re-utilized, like Brandt's New Apollo, would fall under the condemnation ax. Thus, other property owners are not eager to follow the example of the Brandts in undertaking expensive renovation. At the mo-

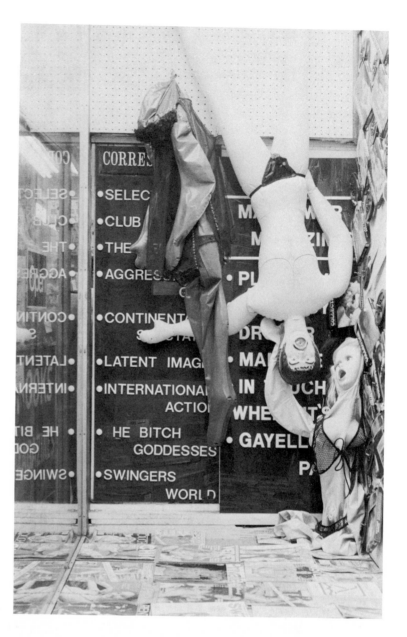

City officials call it visual blight. The customers call it fun.
Daniel Meltzer

ment they feel threatened, not only with the possible loss of their property, but also with the possible loss of further investment were they to upgrade their property. Civic groups are quick to point out that the responsibility for the current atmosphere of decay on Forty-second Street rests with these property owners who allowed their properties to decline.

One sensible alternative to condemnation is offered by Seymour Durst, chairman of the Broadway Association and a Times Square property owner, who favors up-front condemnation of the strip with "city aid being provided to the current landowners for upgrading the existing properties rather than the sale to developers." Under such a plan the present owners who wish to retain their properties would have to upgrade them either by restoration or by razing and new construction and would also have to rid their buildings of objectionable businesses.

While many critics of urban renewal throw the responsibility for redevelopment and cleanup on the shoulders of the Square's current property owners, this may not be the key to any solutions. Many of the owners whose property houses pornographic businesses have neither the need to provide an upgraded environment to attract customers nor the desire to upgrade themselves right out of a profitable rental. Some owners believe that efforts to bring back the middle class to Times Square through better quality will force out the offensive businesses.

The sex emporium—do such institutions attract more people than they offend? **Daniel Meltzer**

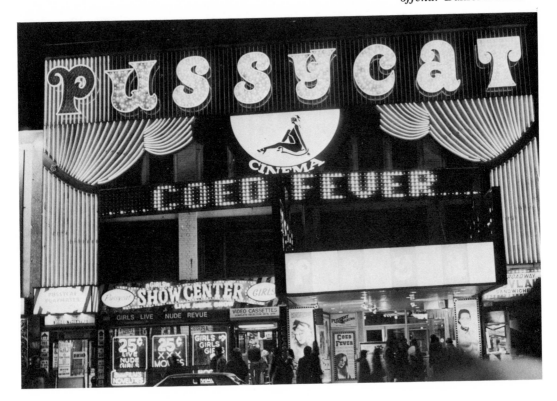

Although the redevelopment of Forty-second Street alone would close down fourteen sex-related businesses, larger businesses like Pussycat and Show World would probably meet with even greater success because of the great numbers of people in the Square, its ease of access, and the anonymity it offers. (The continued existence of a large sex emporium on East Fifty-third Street, in the face of every effort to remove it by the powerful Citicorp, shows that sex-oriented businesses can sustain themselves in upper-income business and shopping areas.)

Sadly, many of the property owners in the Square have ceased caring about its fate. Victims of local street crime and witnesses to the inability of law enforcement agencies to improve these conditions, they have succumbed to the apathy brought on by the deteriorating environment. Individual businesses that have attempted to salvage a property in Times Square have met unlikely opposition from property owners who fail to follow even the simple City ordinance to clean the sidewalks and streets. Special details of federally funded CETA (Comprehensive Employment and Training Act) workers perform the never-ending sanitation work which is too big for the reduced City forces. But the removal of sidewalk litter to the gutters is up to individual shopkeepers, many of whom just leave the litter and scoff at fines and accumulating filth. President Reagan's proposed reduction of funds to such programs as CETA will result in yet further accumulation.

A burnt-out theater marquee on Broadway seemed a simple enough matter to clear away but, months after the fire, the offensive sight remained. A major New York bank held that property as the representative of twelve separate pension trusts whose people didn't "really care," according to the bank. Only after the bank was threatened with newspaper exposure as a slumlord were the charred ruins removed.

Standing by his office window, Robert Brandt will point out the bustle of Forty-second Street below, between Broadway and Eighth Avenue, and

*Welcome to Times
Square.* Daniel Meltzer

discuss the semantic issues of "blight." It is his claim that there is no blight in the form of abandoned, deteriorating architecture on the strip, only the blight of illegal trade taking place openly along both sides of the block. He wistfully proposes emptying *that* block of all street traffic for just an hour so that someone could examine the buildings for structural soundness and judge whether they would be condemned on those grounds. (Structurally, the buildings do appear to be sound, and many still retain their ornate appeal beneath their layer of gaudy posters and advertisements.)

Whether or not the atmosphere would be improved by the removal of "human blight" along the strip is doubtful, but there can be no doubt that the hustlers and peddlers pursuing their various illegal trades from the storefronts offend the middle-class customers the City is so anxious to attract to the area and contribute to an atmosphere of decay and threat. At this point the obvious question asked by any concerned observer is how these illegal street trades came to flourish in this gateway to New York and why they are permitted to stay there, spilling along Eighth Avenue in both directions.

Gerald Schoenfeld of the Shubert Organization asserts that drugs, prostitution, and crime follow logically behind the sex and pornography business. After the relaxation of the laws governing censorship and the definition of pornography in the late 1960s made for booming business in the sex-oriented books, magazines, movies, and live shows, the required space for this trade was readily available in the abandoned storefronts and theaters along Forty-second Street, Eighth Avenue, and Broadway, and the volume of pedestrian traffic passing through the Square made it a desirable location for the growing industry. Times Square was

A "monte man" gathers his audience of marks for a performance of the Forty-second Street hustle. Daniel Meltzer

the traditional spot for show girls and burlesque, further increasing its desirability for any industry built on titillation.

While researching this book, I spent many hours in the Times Square area. There was always a group of policemen at both ends of Forty-second Street between Seventh and Eighth avenues and others in patrol cars, on horseback, and on foot in the immediate area. Times Square never suffered from inadequate police protection—although on several occasions, while I was standing and studying the architectural details, I was advised by the friendlier of New York's Finest that this was not a place for a "lady like you to stand around." It was this advice, more than any actual threats of harm from the people in the street that frightened me the most. It made me feel that the police were powerless to guarantee my safety in the area. It is precisely this impotence, that any policeman who patrols the area will (unofficially) complain of. Constitutional safeguards have severely restricted police efforts to control the street trade, and the frustrated police officers report tales of humiliation at the hands of judges, as the drug peddlers, pimps, prostitutes, and operators of porn parlors walk freely away from City courtrooms. Merchants speak of a "policy of containment"—the assumption being that an unspoken "hands off" agreement on illegal traffic in Times Square prevents its spread onto the side streets where middle-class theatergoers patronize the area's legitimate playhouses. More sinister yet is the theory of some property owners that the area is being allowed to deteriorate in order to ease the urban renewal condemnation process.

Whatever the reason or combination of reasons for the blight, one fact is clear: Unless the obvious threat of hassle and hustle to the average passerby is removed from Forty-second Street, the efforts of any group to renovate structurally will be of little use in cleaning up the area. It is a block that the ordinary citizen avoids, and all New Yorkers are aware of its hazards.

The clutter so prevalent in the streets is reflected in this garish window display offering everything from ghoulish masks to portraits of Christ. Daniel Meltzer

What if merchants cleaned the sidewalks in front of their property and chased away the loiterers? Fred Papert, of the Forty-second Street Development Association, believes that people behave in a manner dictated by their environment and that if the gaudy theater marquees and sex emporiums were replaced by elegant shops, hotels, and theaters, the illegal street trade would no longer be comfortable operating in that environment. This theory is, of course, dependent upon a change in the very nature of the street.

The Forty-second Street Development Association, a nonprofit organization funded largely by the Ford Foundation, is working closely with City agencies, the UDC and other nonprofit groups to develop renewal plans for the entire length of the street stretching west from Times Square to the Hudson River. One possibility being considered by the group is the renovation of the West Side Airlines Terminal. The first three floors would become

An early proposal for the Times Square Mall. Collection of the author

the home for National Recording Studios, with two stories devoted to a television studio and an additional floor of office space above. The fourth floor would be used as a six hundred-seat Off-Broadway Theater.

One of the more exciting proposals is the restoration of the Art Deco McGraw Hill Building on Forty-second Street between Eighth and Ninth avenues. The renovation would emphasize restoration of the decorative exterior, and the interior would be redesigned into quality office and loft space.

The organization is also responsible for a small group of Off-Broadway theaters, known as Theater Row, which have been reclaimed and restored from

One bright spot on the deteriorating western border of the Square is the new Theater Row project of the Forty-second Street Redevelopment Association. Daniel Meltzer

a stretch of dilapidated brownstones along Forty-second Street, west of Ninth Avenue across from Manhattan Plaza—a housing complex for artists, writers, and those connected with New York's performing arts. Theater Row and the City's Manhattan Plaza have brought an energy and vitality to the perimeter of Times Square that has been missing for over half a century.

According to some, the City at Forty-second Street (an offshoot of the Development Association) is a project designed to drive out the current property owners through UDC condemnation procedures or to level the existing properties along the Seventh to Eighth Avenue strip and place the property in the hands of New York's large real estate interests, who will then build glass-and-steel skyscrapers housing offices, hotels, theaters, and shops. This is obviously the view of the owners along the strip, but it is also the view of many theater owners in the area who object to such plans on the grounds that they will destroy the scale of the area.

Mr. Papert will freely admit that some large office

structures are necessary to carry the tax burden but paints a different picture of the fate of existing property. The brochure describing plans for the Seventh to Eighth Avenue project known as the City at Forty-second Street incorporates the existing structures in its framework (but neglects to mention under whose ownership).

The City at Forty-second Street is a 750,000-square-foot complex proposed for the Seventh and Eighth Avenue blocks of

Originally planned as upper-income housing at Tenth Avenue, Manhattan Plaza is now home to artists and theater people. Daniel Meltzer

Forty-second Street. This project would build on the existing assets of the area—its history, its architecture, its extraordinary accessibility, the purchasing power of the 200,000 people who daily rush to get away from its present blight—with the restoration of a half a dozen of the street's legendary theaters and the creation on a mezzanine level above them, a complex of exhibits and retail/restaurant atriums which, in sum, would celebrate cities. It would serve as a gateway to New York, an information center, arts, communication and entertainment center, a launching pad for city visitors. The project will be organized around a spacious concourse which will bridge Forty-second Street in three locations.

They specifically list the preservation of the New Amsterdam, Selwyn, Harris, Victory, and Apollo—restoring their use as legitimate theaters. Also restored will be the facades of the Times Square, Lyric, and Empire.

These plans, however, suffered a setback when Mayor Edward I. Koch threw open the redevelopment of Forty-second Street, permitting private developers to submit their own plans. It is the stated goal of the New York City Planning Commission to "turn Times Square into the world's greatest entertainment district."

Today's refurbished Shubert Alley, center of a revitalized theater district. **Daniel Meltzer**

The City at Forty-second Street is responsible for one new landmark on the Times Square scene. Artist Richard Haas has transformed the cinderblock wall of the Crossroads Building (on the south side of Forty-second Street, opposite the triangle) into a magnificent mural of the old Times Tower which stood opposite the location of the new mural.

The TKTS booth at Duffy Square, where last-minute seats to Broadway's hits and flops are sold at half-price. **Daniel Meltzer**

Another project designed to revitalize the ailing Square is raising the ire of theatrical interests, preservationists, and private enterprise. For some time now there have been plans for a luxurious hotel to be built on Broadway between Forty-fifth and Forty-sixth streets. The massive Portman Hotel would be built at a cost of $260 million and would considerably boost the tourist trade that has sought lodging in safer, more luxurious sites outside the immediate Times Square area. The Shubert Organization, owners of at least seventeen Times Square theaters, views the hotel as the giant step necessary to reverse the declining trend in the Square.

However, the owners of the Picadilly Hotel, which currently stands on the site and waits for the condemnation ax to fall, have gone to court in an attempt to stop the use of federal money to condemn their hotel.

The Portman project is also opposed by landmark advocates and Actors Equity because it means the loss of three of Times Square's most beautiful and well-known theaters: the Helen Hayes, Morosco,

A painting of the old Times Tower by artist Richard Haas now graces the Crossroads Building. **Jacob Burckhardt**

and Bijou. The City's position (pro-Portman) is that the loss of the three theaters will be offset by the construction of a new legitimate theater in the hotel which in turn will encourage the revitalization of the older movie houses in Times Square and return them to their original use as legitimate stages. The opposition cries that theaters like the proposed house incorporated in the Portman plans are "barns" and that, while encouragement to revitalize the older theaters should continue, there is still no adequate reason to lose the three in question.

One area landmark dating back to the turn of the century, remains on the corner of Broadway and Forty-second Street. Although its original ornate facade can be seen only several stories above street level, under the modernized window displays below lies the Knickerbocker Hotel, now converted to office space. The Helmsley Corporation, one of New York's largest real-estate interests, has announced plans to restore the Knickerbocker to livable space by its conversion to combination office and living quarters with a price tag of $1,000 to $2,000 per month—a very high rent for living space in an area as "blighted" as Times Square. This announcement would indicate a rather strong assurance, from one of the City's real-estate giants, that within a short time Times Square will be habitable for affluent tenants.

Other plans for the development of the west side surrounding Forty-second Street remain controversial. A mammoth apparel mart designed to link the prosperous garment district more closely to the Square was a part of the plan created by the City at Forty-second Street and recently set aside by Mayor Koch.

All the recent City administrations have proclaimed the cleanup of Times Square as a goal of the City government yet, previously, little had been done toward that end. Now, however, despite the infighting among the interests in the Square, painfully slow progress is finally taking place.

For those of us who are detached from the political and economic intricacies of the situation, it is obvious that a simple, commonsense approach to law enforcement and the development of the area is needed to break the stalemate that's perpetuating decline. Richard Basini, executive director of the Broadway Association, explains:

> By now it should be patently clear that the movement to revitalize Times Square has degenerated from a state of analysis into one of paralysis. Instead of taking small pragmatic steps to rescue this treasured district, we have settled for a decade of city-funded, myriad studies in search of the grand solution. The solution is first to enforce the existing laws and zoning regulations, thus making the area unwelcome for the street people while, at the same time, encouraging much-wanted development.

Perhaps such solid ideas are now too simple for the complex war raging between community groups, planners, investors, developers, politicians, and property owners.

Yet it would appear that these groups have finally awakened to a fact that any one of Times Square's millions of tourists could have told them long ago. Times Square is at the very heart of New York. To every serviceman, family, visiting dignitary, star-struck newcomer to Broadway, and out-of-towner-turned-New Yorker, the City is Times Square, and the conditions there mirror the condition of the

For a sailor on leave, it's still a pretty girl and a tour of Times Square.
Daniel Meltzer

George M. Cohan's statue stands watch over the greatest entertainment center in the world. Daniel Meltzer

City. If we love New York as much as we advertise we do, why have we let its greatest single landmark come to ruin?

Whatever the outcome of the battle over Times Square, it seems obvious that its life has always depended on the entertainment industry. From the moment Oscar Hammerstein pioneered on the Longacre with his Olympia Theater, it was the Broadway boards, the Hollywood extravaganzas, the nightclubs, and the fine restaurants of Times Square that drew the crowds of adoring fans, visitors, officials, mobsters, teenagers, showgirls, tourists, and socialites to that tiny internationally famous triangle. The City Planning Commission wants to "turn Times Square into a great entertainment center" but it has forgotten something: The Commissioners need only to glance back for a moment at the decades of glorious history to know their goal should be to *return* Times Square to the greatest entertainment center in the world.

Index

Index **175**